The Christian
and Good Mental Health

by Larry T. Swaim, Th.D.,
LPC, CMFT ret.

ISBN: 978-0-89098-877-0

©2017 by 21st Century Christian

2809 12th Ave S, Nashville, TN 37204

All rights reserved.

Unless otherwise noted Scripture quotations are from the New King James Version.

Scripture taken from the New King James Version.

Copyright © 1982 by Thomas Nelson, Inc. Used by permission. All rights reserved.

Cover design by Jonathan Edelhuber

ACKNOWLEDGMENTS

I wish to thank
Suzanne Galford, my daughter,
and Cathy Brown,
for their valuable help
in editing and proofreading.

DEDICATIONS

To my parents,
Tom and Imogene Swaim,
who supplied
the early foundation for my faith.

TABLE OF CONTENTS

INTRODUCTION

For the committed Christian, locating competent mental health professionals who are committed to Christian values and principles is becoming increasingly difficult. Our permissive, secular culture has infiltrated almost every discipline, and mental health is no exception. Mental health providers who have little or no spiritual or moral values can often do more harm than good, and certainly from a spiritual point of view can lead a person in a direction away from Christ and His teachings.

I believe that good mental health treatment and maintaining spiritual values are compatible, and that a person does not have to compromise one to receive the other. But even among those who are Christian therapists, there are varying degrees of spiritual commitment. A client or patient must be willing to ask the right questions in the beginning to know if his therapist is a good fit for his mental and spiritual health. Make a list of what is important to you spiritually. Don't be afraid to ask a therapist her thoughts on those various spiritual values. Keep an open mind, but also be willing to question any suggestions or advice that you may feel compromises your spiritual ideas and values. Seldom will we ever find anyone who agrees with us on everything spiritually, so it is important to define what is most important to you and let those principles be your guideline for selecting a competent therapist.

This book is designed primarily to get an overview of some of the most common mental and emotional illnesses and disorders.

Descriptions and definitions along with symptoms and treatment possibilities are suggested for each chapter. At the end of the book, there is a hotline and information lines for those who are in crisis. These phone numbers will assist you in receiving information or critical help in times of depression, anxiety, grief, or other mental or emotional crises. It is my sincere prayer that this book will be of assistance to Christians seeking guidance and direction for developing and maintaining good mental health.

It would be difficult, if not impossible, to discuss every mental or emotional condition listed in the *Diagnostic and Statistical Manual* used by mental health professionals. But I have selected those that I have most often seen in my practice over the last thirty years.

During a mental health emergency, one should seek the closest mental health professional for immediate assistance. Long-term therapy decisions can be made at a later time, when the patient is not in crisis.

CHAPTER 1

AN OVERVIEW OF MENTAL AND EMOTIONAL DISORDERS

Biblical Example

Those whose lives are portrayed for us in the Bible from Old and New Testament times are basically no different than we are. They struggled with the same difficulties, emotional problems, stresses, and temptations each of us does. Some were more successful than others in trying to live according to God's will. We sometimes think that, because thousands of years have passed since the beginning of the Old and New Testament eras, we are somehow different today from our predecessors. The truth is that we still struggle with all of the same problems, difficulties, and temptations that they did. As we progress through this book, developing an understanding of mental and emotional problems, we will come to realize that even in biblical times, though not diagnosed as we are today, many people struggled with the same emotional and mental illnesses that we do. It could be said that Paul, Peter, Judas, Cornelius, King Saul, Moses, David, Solomon, Mary and Martha, Noah, and others struggled with what could be defined as mental or emotional illnesses for varying lengths of time and degree during their lives. Mankind has always struggled to think rightly and often gone in directions that lead to mental problems. The answer to dealing with these difficulties and problems is depending on the grace and mercy of God, changing what we can and, with God's help, accepting what we cannot change. Jesus, our perfect example, teaches us how to accept the will of God when it may not be our own desire or will and how to accept the circumstances that come our way that we cannot change.

One in three people will have a significant mental or emotional problem during their lifetime. If this were any other illness, we would call it epidemic. The Bible says "As [a man] thinks in his heart or mind, so is he" (Proverbs 23:7, NKJV). What we put into our mind and the thought patterns we develop affect our behavior.

Sometimes we allow ourselves to be programmed incorrectly. A thought goes in, becomes confused or abnormal, and we repeat that thought pattern over and over again, receiving the same incorrect results. When this happens we have what is called an abnormal thought pattern. Some mental illness is a result of incorrect thought patterns.

Most of us at one time or another have some minor emotional or mental struggles. They may not rise to the level of being called a mental or emotional illness, but it is an emotional mental struggle. Approximately 60 million Americans experience some type of mental emotional problem each year. Mental illness is defined as "any various psychiatric condition usually characterized by impairment of an individual's normal cognitive (how we think, what we think about, how we develop our minds, attention, language, perception, problem solving, creativity) and emotional behavior functions that are caused by psychological or psycho-social factors" (Mayo Clinic). Another definition of mental or emotional illness is "a broadly inclusive term generally denoting one or all of the following: a disease of the brain with predominant behavior symptoms such as paresis (a partial paralysis), acute alcoholism, a disease of the mind, a disease of the personality, as evidenced by abnormal behavior such as hysteria, schizophrenia, also called on occasion emotional disease or disturbance or behavioral problems and behavioral illness" (National Alliance on Mental Illness).

Numbers of Americans Affected by Mental Illness

* One in four adults, approximately 61.5 million Americans, experiences mental illness in a given year. One in 17, about 13.6 million, live with a serious mental illness such as schizophrenia, major depression, or bipolar disorder.

* Approximately 20 percent of youth ages 13 to 18 experience severe mental disorders in a given year. For ages 8 to 15, the estimate is 13 percent.

* Approximately 1.1 percent of American adults, about 2.4 million people, live with schizophrenia.

* Approximately 2.6 percent of American adults, 6.1 million people, live with bipolar disorder.

* Approximately 6.7 percent of American adults, about 14.8 million people, live with major depression.

* Approximately 18.1 percent of American adults, about 42 million people, live with anxiety disorders, such as panic disorder, obsessive-compulsive disorder (OCD), post-traumatic stress disorder (PTSD), generalized anxiety disorder and phobias.

* About 9.2 million adults have co-occurring mental health and addiction disorders.

* Approximately 26 percent of homeless adults staying in shelters live with serious mental illness, and an estimated 46 percent live with mental illness and/or substance abuse disorders.

* Approximately 20 percent of state prisoners and 21 percent of local jail prisoners have "a recent history" of a mental health condition.

* Seventy percent of youth in juvenile justice systems have at least one mental health condition, and at least 20 percent of those youth live with a several mental illness.

Getting Mental Health Treatment in America

* Approximately 60 percent of adults and almost one-half of youth ages 8-15 with a mental illness received no mental health services in the previous year.

* African Americans and Hispanic Americans used mental health services at about one-half the rate of whites in the past year and Asian Americans at about one-third the rate.

* One-half of all chronic mental illness begins by the age of 14; three-quarters by age 24. Despite effective treatment, there are long delays—sometimes decades—between the first appearance of symptoms and when people get help.

The Impact of Mental Illness in America

* Serious mental illness costs America $193.2 billion in lost earnings per year.

* Mood disorders such as depression are the third most com-mon cause of hospitalization in the U.S. for both youth and adults ages 18 to 44.

* Individuals living with serious mental illness face an increased risk of having chronic medical conditions. Adults living with serious mental illness die on average 25 years earlier than other Americans, largely due to treatable medical conditions.

* Over 50 percent of students with a mental health condition age 14 and older who are served by special education drop out—the highest dropout rate of any disability group.

* Suicide is the tenth leading cause of death in the U.S., more common than homicide and the third leading cause of death for ages 15 to 24 years. More than 90 percent of those who die by suicide had one or more mental disorders.

* Although military members comprise less than 1 percent of the U.S. population, veterans represent 20 percent of

suicides nationally. Each day, about 22 veterans die from suicide. (Source: *Psychology Today*)

We often attach a stigma to mental or emotional disorders that we would not attach to physical illnesses or disorders. Some people feel, as Job's friends did, that we must have done or thought something rising to the level of a sin to result in our having a financial loss, or an emotional or mental problem, or a serious significant physical illness. We know, of course, that such thinking is certainly not true. It is true that some mental and emotional problems are the result of bad choices, just like some physical injuries with which we have to live for a lifetime are results of bad choices. We are not the ones who can judge adequately what is or is not the result of bad choices. Since all of us are poor choosers, we cannot and must not unduly judge anyone for the circumstances of their life. Judging is God's business, not ours. Accepting and loving people as they are, regardless of what circumstances may have brought them there, is our responsibility.

What we need is a type of "hospital church," where anyone who is in need, anyone who is hurting or desperate, anyone who feels abandoned, thrown away, or misunderstood, can find a fellowship of God's people who will encourage and help them and, if nothing else, just listen to them. Catharsis, the art of releasing emotional pain, often just by talking it out, is one of the most important and valuable tools of therapy. There are millions of people who do not need anything more than someone to listen and to acknowledge that their problems are real—someone to feel a little sympathy and empathy for them. Yet many with emotional problems are unable to find such friends. It may be that some people who are classified as emotionally ill are simply lonely. Because of that loneliness, they can become confused and are unable to get feedback because there is no one who cares enough to listen. When we talk with friends like this, we do not need to offer advice. We need only to listen. As Christians, we must be willing to invest time and effort in our friends, our brothers and sisters in Christ, to help bring them to where they need to be. Christians have a responsibility to every hurting person who crosses their path—everyone—and we have a responsibility to help them in whatever way we can. And for most of us, it's just being a good listener. God may allow us to cross paths with the needy as He did with the Ethiopian eunuch or Esther. Each of us has talents and abilities and opportunities. Esther had an opportunity, which she seized and, with the help of God, was able to save her nation. We have great opportunities, and when we take advantage of them with God's blessings and help, we can do great things as well. If we can help just one person, then we have done well.

Learning to Live With the Problem

We would like to eliminate our physical, mental, and emotional illnesses and disabilities. But the reality is that some of us will have to live with some of these conditions. Many will have to learn to cope with their mental and emotional illnesses, just as some must learn to live blind, deaf, crippled, or disfigured, and some will have to learn to live with debilitating physical diseases. Christians as well as non-Christians can have emotional problems. There should be no stigma or guilt attached to such illnesses. The church should be loving, compassionate, and helpful. Unfortunately, not all members of the church are mature enough to accept and encourage those who are mentally ill. I attended a church once where one of the ladies in our congregation had a significant mental illness. She would often have bouts of depression that would bring her to the brink of suicide. She was in and out of the local mental hospital. After being released from the hospital on one occasion, she came to church and was sitting near the back. During the service, she had an episode that resulted in calling attention to her problem. Some of the members of the congregation began to snicker and laugh, turning around and looking as if they were disgusted, even repulsed. Sad to say, she never returned to our congregation. There should be no stigma attached to mental illness. As brothers and sisters in Christ, we should be understanding and compassionate, just as Jesus never ridiculed, made fun of, or judged those who suffered with mental or emotional problems.

Brief History of Care For the Mentally Ill

The first asylum was built in the fourth century in Baghdad. The next one was built in Cairo, Egypt in 872 AD. Concerned followers of Jesus built several mental health facilities in Spain, the first one in 1245 AD, the second one in 1436 AD in Seville, Spain. More were constructed—in 1481 in Barcelona, and in 1483 in Toledo. Jumping 300 years, in 1808 one of the first asylums for the mentally ill was built in London, England.

In most parts of the world, as far back as history can go, the mentally ill were cared for by families and friends. When mental institutions began to develop, they were mainly warehouses for the insane. Many of those confined were abused. There was very little hygiene and almost no treatment. In the United States, beginning in the late 1800s, there were a number of mental institutions built. By 1904, there was a significant population in mental institutions. There was much experimenting done on the mentally ill. Experiments involving lobotomies, electric shock, insulin shock, and for those who could not be significantly improved, there was forced sterilization.

Beginning in the early 1950s, lawsuits began to be brought against those owning and operating mental institutions citing inhumane treatment, and there were demands for improvement. Simultaneously, new drugs were being developed to help stabilize many of those with the most common mental conditions. Eventually legislation was enacted, and it was no longer against the law to be "crazy." You could not be confined against your will to a mental institution unless you were judged to be criminally insane or you were a continuing threat to yourself or someone else. By the late 1950s and early 1960s, many of these mental health institutions were being closed. Today, most of the larger hospitals have floors devoted to helping the mentally ill, or there are small freestanding additions to our hospitals dedicated to the mentally ill. The length of time a person may be held against his will in a mental facility ranges from 48 to 72 hours, not including weekends. Without a court order in which they must be adjudged by a mental health professional and/or judge to be an immediate threat to themselves or someone else, they cannot be held for a longer period of time.

The High Cost of Mental Illness

The cost of mental and emotional illness is extremely high. Those who are depressed and anxious and those who have even more serious mental disorders will tell you it's like living in hell. The anguish and pain is beyond description, and most would do any reasonable thing to get rid of the black cloud that engulfs them. The cost to the individual's happiness, peace of mind, and purpose is higher than we could ever imagine. And there is a cost to their families as well, who must care for those who are mentally or emotionally ill. Many parents, husbands, and wives must put their own lives on hold, put aside their own desires to travel or to enjoy their hobbies, so that they can take care of their mentally ill relatives or close friends. These caregivers often experience much of the pain and suffering that those they care for feel. The truth is, Christians are not immune to mental or emotional diseases any more than they are immune to cancer or any other physical disease or disability, and neither are those who care for them immune from the responsibility and the opportunity of showing true Christian love and care.

The costs go even further than that, however. The incredible financial cost both to the individual and family as well as to the health care cost to the nation are staggering. An article in the January/February 2015 issue of *Foreign Affairs* chronicles the hidden cost of global mental illness. The article is authored by Thomas R. Insel, Pamela Y. Collins, and Stephen E. Hyman. "In 2010, the report's authors found non-communicable disease caused 63% of all deaths around the world, and 80% of those fatalities occurred in countries that are characterized as low income or middle income... But the report contains one big surprise. It predicted that the largest source of future costs would be mental disorders, which the report forecast would account for more than a third of the global economy burden of non-communicable diseases by the year 2030. Taken together, the direct economic effects of mental illness (such as spending on care) and the indirect effects (lost productivity) already cost the global economy around 2.5 trillion dollars a year. By 2030, the team projects most amounts will increase to around 6 trillion in constant dollars, more than heart disease and cancer and diabetes and respiratory illnesses all combined.... In wealthy countries most people continue to view mental illness as a problem facing individuals and families rather than a policy change challenge with significant economic and political implications... In reality, in countries of all levels of wealth and development, mental illness affects almost every aspect of society and economy, and far from lacking relevance or urgency in poor or war-torn countries, mental illness often contributes to the very dysfunctions that plague such places... Mental disorders are far more disabling than most people realize, often preventing the afflicted from working, studying, caring for others, producing, and consuming. In a 2012 report on the global economy burden of disease, the World Health Organization noted that mental illness and behavioral disorders account for 26% of time lost to disability, more than any other disease. The World Health Organization estimates that some 800,000 people commit suicide every year. Globally, more than twice as many people die from suicide as die from homicide each year. And suicide is the second largest source of mortality for people between the ages of 15 to 29, topped only by traffic accidents. Globally, in low income countries, up to 85% of the people with severe mental illnesses will receive no treatment at all." Truly the cost of mental illness is high in every area.

Questions

1. What does the way we think have to do with who we are and how we behave?

2. Does what we allow ourselves to think affect our behavior and mental health?

3. How many Americans experience some type of mental or emotional problem each year? Why do you think the number is so high?

4. Do Americans with mental and emotional problems receive adequate treatment? If not, why not?

5. Why do you think there is such a high suicide rate in the United States? What more can we do to reduce this number?

6. Is there a stigma to mental or emotional disorders in our society today? Is there a stigma in the church?

7. As God's people, how can we best help those who are mentally and emotionally ill?

8. When was the first asylum in recorded history built?

9. Throughout history, who has been responsible for most of the care of the mentally ill?

10. How can we learn to live with sicknesses and illnesses we cannot change?

CHAPTER 2

AS A MAN THINKS:
DEVELOPING GOOD THOUGHT PATTERNS

Proverbs 23:7, "For as he thinks in his heart, so is he" (NKJV). Thoughts cause feelings, and feelings cause actions; this is a truism known by psychologists and first revealed in the Bible. Thoughts produce feelings or emotions, and emotions produce action. Emotions help us survive by preparing us for danger or threats. Emotions have to do with the internal parts that are motivated to help us survive by withdrawing from a threat, running toward a threat, or hiding from the threat. When we express our emotion in terms of actions, then we have what is called "affect"; that is, a difference in our facial expressions and our actions. Our emotions usually have predictable patterns, which can be easily recognized and transmitted without words to another, simply by seeing our expressions. We can usually tell how a person is feeling by noticing his "affect." One example would be if a person has a sad countenance, looking down, teary-eyed, we would probably recognize that the person is sad or depressed. The affect of the eyes is revealing concerning the condition of the mind and soul. The expression, "The eyes are the windows of the soul" was first penned by Shakespeare in the play *Richard III*. I believe that mental and emotional illness can sometimes be detected in the eyes. There are sad eyes, empty eyes, angry eyes, hopeless eyes, fearful eyes, lost eyes—all of these give us a peek into the condition of the mind and the soul. Jesus, in the Sermon on the Mount, says, "The eye is the lamp of the body. So, if your eye is healthy, your whole body will be full of light, but if your eye is bad, your whole body will be full of darkness. If the light in you is darkness, how great is the darkness!" (Matthew 6:22, 23, ESV). I hope you never have to become acquainted with words like *lugubrious, catatonic, crestfallen,* or *blunted* !

Emotions are essential, both in terms of catharsis (releasing often by talking our feelings out) as well as in meeting social and physical needs. James Coggin, M.D., physician and lecturer, lists three reasons why emotions are essential:

(1) Emotions focus our attention on important things that affect our social safety and well-being;

(2) emotions motivate us to do whatever we need to do about things to get what we want or need;

(3) emotions cause physiological changes in the body, like breathing and heart rate, to allow us to do what we need to do.

Emotions can either be positive or negative. Positive emotions, like pleasure, happiness, and joy, arise out of good things as we perceive them happening in our lives. Negative feelings come from what we perceive to be threats or dangers to us. Each day is filled with both positive and negative emotions. Paul Ekman lists six basic emotions. All but one are negative: fear, anger, sadness, disgust, surprise, and contentment or happiness.

"People are disturbed not by things, but by their perception of things" (Epictetus, a Greek Stoic philosopher). Thoughts can be either real or imagined. In fact, the imagined thoughts are just as helpful or harmful as the real ones. Perception is reality to the body and mind. Our thoughts control our emotions, which in turn controls our mood, and finally our actions. Our mood may change several times during the day, from feeling threatened, to feeling secure, to feeling happy or a sense of well-being. What we think is quite important. It controls our emotions, the chemistry and hormones of our body, and can dramatically help in making us sick or well. Scripture advises us about how we should think:

> "...do not be anxious about anything, but in everything by prayer and supplication with thanksgiving let your requests be made known to God. And the peace of God, which surpasses all understanding, will guard your hearts and your minds in Christ Jesus. Finally, brothers, whatever is true, whatever is honorable, whatever is just, whatever is pure, whatever is lovely, whatever is commendable, if there is any excellence, if there is anything worthy of praise, think about these things" (Philippians 4:6-8, ESV).

By thinking positive, good thoughts, we become positive and better. The 16th-century philosopher/scientist Rene Descartes is renowned for his statement, "I think, therefore I am."

Memory

Memory has emotional attachments. You've likely experienced this when remembering a loved one who has died. Our memories evoke emotional feelings. Because of this emotional attachment, take care to think no evil. We must control our thoughts, make them as productive and positive as possible, expecting the best, yet preparing to deal with the worst. Thoughts cause emotions, emotions cause actions—good or bad—depending on how we translate those thoughts in our mind. Our thoughts produce psychosomatic reactions; that is, mind-body reactions. Our thoughts actually affect our physical, mental, and spiritual well-being. And just a word about faith here: Faith is essential in dealing with many of the problems and difficulties that confront us in our life. Faith in God, faith in Jesus as His Son, faith in His Word as inspired and infallible, and faith in His watchful care and protection of us. This is the reason I favor faith-based hospitals, faith-based physicians, doctors who pray before they go into surgery, faith-based psychologists and psychiatrists. I believe that faith in God is one of the most powerful thoughts, feelings, and emotions we can have.

One reality is that what we put in our minds becomes that to which we react or act upon. Simply put, what we feed grows; what we starve dies. Therefore, if we think on good things, we become better. If we think on evil, bad thoughts, we will become more and more evil. The concept extends beyond our thoughts. If an alcoholic feeds his addiction with alcohol, he will get worse. If a drug addict feeds on drugs of choice, he will get worse. If a sex addict watches pornography and feeds on pornographic magazines or websites, he will get worse. However, if you starve anything harmful, you will get stronger and better. Resultingly, you will have a more balanced and happier life. Peace of mind and happiness are worthy goals, but seldom achieved when we harbor the wrong kinds of thoughts. To be truly *happy* and *content*, we must control our thinking. To be *mentally healthy*, we must be able to control our thinking. Thinking positive, good thoughts produces a sense of security, contentment, and happiness because,

"As a man thinks, so is he" (Proverbs 23:7, KJV).

The Mind Has Similarities to a Computer

Our mind is similar to a computer. Your input determines your output. How foolish it would be to say, "I hate this computer. It never gives me the right answer!" Even if you have the most sophisticated, powerful computer in the world, it will give you incorrect information and will never function properly if you program it incorrectly. Some computers can be attacked by various viruses that can distort or destroy our files, compromising the information that has been input. Sometimes these viruses even infect our friends' computers as we communicate with one another. When we allow hurtful thoughts, words, actions, and even deeds to fill our mind, it causes wrong thinking and even unintended consequences. Actually, there is a great need to renew our minds from time to time, to go through a cleansing process of our habits and thought patterns, taking a self inventory and making sure that what we're putting in our minds is helpful and productive. Ephesians 4:23 encourages us to "be renewed in the spirit of your mind." We need to forget how we used to be when we were not thinking correctly, forget about our sins and mistakes, forgive and forget what others have done to us, and develop the fruit of the Spirit "love, joy, peace, patience, kindness, goodness, faithfulness, gentleness, self-control" (Galatians 5:22-23, ESV).

If you think sad thoughts, you will become sad. If you think angry thoughts, you will be angry and possibly hurt yourself and others. But if you think positive, good, right, kind thoughts, you will be happy and a blessing to yourself and others. Choose to think positively. Again, Scripture teaches us: "Finally, brothers, whatever is true, whatever is honorable, whatever is just, whatever is pure, whatever is lovely, whatever is commendable, if there is any excellence, if there is anything worthy of praise, think about these things" (Philippians 4:8). This Scripture bears repeating. You can have peace of mind, peace in your heart, and peace with your friends, if you think peacefully.

When you are facing problems, don't give up. Sometimes we relapse and go back to our old way of thinking. Galatians 6:9 says, "Let us not grow weary while doing good." We will have opposition in trying to live a positive, helpful, and righteously minded life. There will be people who do not understand and who will even criticize and condemn our way of thinking as being naïve. But as we are told in Hebrews 12:3, "Consider Him who endured such hostility from sinners…lest you become weary and discouraged in your souls." I like Colossians 3:2, "Set your mind on things above, not on things on the earth."

Our Best Psychology Book
The Bible is the best psychology book ever written. It tells us how to have a sound mind. Jesus is the Great Physician. He tells us how to heal our mind, body, and soul. He gives us grace to change

what we can, to accept what we cannot, and the wisdom to know the difference. The "Serenity Prayer" is truly a Christian prayer. If you change your thoughts, you will change your life. I am not denying that there are chemical, biological, genetic, and hormonal considerations to how we think, but the one thing we have the most control over in dealing with our thinking is choosing what we think about and how we think—positive or negative. I read of a man whose business card read, "The way to happiness: Keep your heart free from hate, your mind free from worry, live simply, expect little, give much, fill your life with love, scatter sunshine, forget self, think of others, do to others what you want done to you." That's a pretty good philosophy to live by.

Isaiah 55:7 admonishes, "Let the wicked forsake his way." It isn't enough just to put away evil. We must replace the evil we have done with good. William James, who is said to be the father of American psychology, said, "The greatest discovery of my generation is that human beings can alter their lives by altering their attitude of mind." And that's what God said first: "As a man thinks, so is he" (Proverbs 23:7, KJV).

The Attitudes of Christ

"Blessed are the poor in spirit, for theirs is the kingdom of heaven.

Blessed are those who mourn, for they shall be comforted.

Blessed are the meek, for they shall inherit the earth.

Blessed are those who hunger and thirst for righteousness, for they shall be satisfied.

Blessed are the merciful, for they shall receive mercy.

Blessed are the pure in heart, for they shall see God.

Blessed are the peacemakers, for they shall be called sons of God.

Blessed are those who are persecuted for righteousness' sake, for theirs is the kingdom of heaven.

Blessed are you when others revile you and persecute you and utter all kinds of evil against you falsely on my account. Rejoice and be glad, for your reward is great in heaven, for so they persecuted the prophets who were before you"
(Matthew 5:2-11, ESV).

We can't control everything, but we can control our thoughts!

Questions

1. How can our affect reveal something about our emotional state?
2. Are emotions necessary? If so, why?
3. What are three reasons why emotions are essential?
4. What are the two types of emotions?
5. What are the six basic emotions?
6. Can our emotions be affected by what we think, whether real or imagined?
7. Does memory affect our emotions?
8. What are some ways we can control our emotions by controlling our thoughts?
9. What is the best psychology book ever written and why?
10. Jesus enumerated the beautiful attitudes we need to develop. What are they?

CHAPTER 3

ANXIETY

Biblical Example

When we read in the Bible about Jesus' experiences in the Garden of Gethsemane prior to His trials and crucifixion, we see an almost perfect example of how to handle the most debilitating anxiety. At this point in the evening, the Passover meal was complete, and Jesus and His disciples had gone to the garden. Leaving some of His companions at the entrance, Jesus went further in with Peter, James, and John. According to Luke, Jesus then left these last three disciples, going about a stone's throw away to be by Himself and pray. "[He] in every respect has been tempted as we are, yet without sin" (Hebrews 4:15, ESV). And here in the garden, as He anticipates His arrest, trials, and crucifixion, Jesus begins to feel the human trait of anxiety. He falls to His knees and prays to the Father that if it be possible, this cup might pass from Him; that if there is any other way for man to be redeemed, that it might be so. But then Jesus gives us one of the keys to overcoming anxiety. "Not my will, but yours, be done" (Luke 22:42, ESV). God knew what was best for Jesus and for us. The confidence that Jesus had in the Father's will being done is an indication of how we should face our difficulties, trials, and tribulations.

Luke, the medical doctor, describes what happened to Jesus as He prayed so fervently (he uses the words "in agony") that sweat drops as blood began to flow down His face. Out of all of the gospel writers, only Luke M.D. describes this condition, called *heratidrosis*. It results in the excretion of blood or blood pigment in the sweat under conditions of great emotional stress. The capillaries in the sweat glands can rupture, as a result mixing blood with perspiration. This is truly an exaggerated form of anxiety. Though rare, it is sometimes experienced by those in the depths of acute anxiety.

As Jesus faced the greatest test of His life, He did what each one of us should do when faced with great distress and anxiety. He sought the will of the Father, and He placed himself completely at the disposal of the Father's will. What an incredibly stressful period it must have been for Him, knowing that heaven or hell were at stake for humanity and that without God's justice being met man could never experience salvation. But the human side of Him longed to be free from the curse of death. After understanding that the Father's will should and must be done, Jesus got up and walked back to the sleeping apostles, wondering why they could not even watch for an hour while He prayed. The moment He saw the mob, led by Judas, coming to arrest Him, He conceded fully to the will of God. He now faced His final hours on earth with confidence and trust.

When we reach the point in our lives when we can honestly and completely say, "Not my will by your will be done, Father," life or death, sickness or health, poverty or wealth, marriage or celibacy, then we will be at the point of controlling and often eliminating the anxieties that come our way.

No one is exempt from fear, anxiety, or worry. We all have problems that flood our minds and cause us to wonder at times if we can survive. The Bible teaches us, "...do not be anxious about anything, but in everything by prayer and supplication with thanksgiving let your requests be made known to God. And the peace of God, which surpasses all understanding, will guard your hearts and your minds in Christ Jesus" (Philippians 4: 6, 7, ESV). Forty million Americans suffer annually from anxiety. Anxiety is defined as "a feeling of distress experienced as fear or worry. It is expressed through a variety of autonomic and central nervous system responses." Anxiety affects the entire body. When I was younger, it was not called anxiety. People were said to have a "nervous breakdown." I remember my mother saying, "If you children don't straighten up, I'm going to have a nervous breakdown!" What she was saying was that she was anxious, and that we children were part of her anxiety.

A Thorough Physical Check-Up

Anxiety often causes one to hyperventilate, feeling as if you can't catch your breath or breathe normally, or to have severe chest pain as if you were having a heart attack. The word *anxiety* is derived from the Latin word *angere*. Translated into English, it means "to strangle or choke." A person feels a tightness in his throat and chest. Diagnosing the exact cause of these feelings is often difficult and should begin with a physical examination because there are physical conditions with the same or similar symptoms as anxiety. Such physical conditions include hyperthyroidism, lupus, hormonal imbalances, hypoglycemia (a condition involving low blood sugar, which can make one feel dizzy, irritable, shaky, and confused), mitral valve prolapse, and Meniere's syndrome (an inner ear problem involving vertigo, dizziness, and feelings of anxiety). Any of these diseases or disorders can create symptoms similar to an assumed stress-related anxiety or panic attack.

Sleep is essential to good mental health. Sleep deprivation precedes anxiety 30 percent of the time. Sleep deprivation precedes depression 69 percent of the time. Good sleep is vitally important.

In simpler terms, anxiety is the mind's way of saying, "Something isn't right." There is danger, fear, or stress posing a threat to us. With all anxiety, brain chemistry changes. It is the fight or flight syndrome that causes an infusion of adrenalin and dopamine. Every part of the body is affected by anxiety, and anxiety is the most common of all emotional and mental disorders. Anxiety is primarily about the possibility of losing control. Major feelings are involved with anxiety. One is loss. You are afraid that you will lose something important to you. It may be your life or your health. The fear of death is the most common of all fears. Or it may be fear of losing your possessions or a friendship or other relationship. It may be fear of losing a loved one. Often we are overwhelmed with a fear of loss. However important that loss is to us is how acute the anxiety will be. We may begin to fear, worry about, or stress over every situation.

Anxiety is perfectly normal. Everyone should experience some anxiety at some point in their life because there are legitimate dangers and situations that pose a threat to us and should cause anxiety.

Generalized anxiety causes us to feel the same feeling of threat or loss with many problems and situations, most of which do not pose a threat to us. Generalized anxiety is a painful condition. It can affect your health and well-being. Studies have shown that it affects the heart and other internal organs. It affects the entire nervous system. We are not meant to live under constant anxiety. Anxiety is meant for specific times and places, but it is not where we are supposed to live.

Normal anxiety occurs, for example, when the phone rings at 3 am. Normal anxiety occurs when you are driving to work and there is a traffic jam, causing you to be late. There are all kinds of minor stressors in our lives that cause a temporary condition of anxiety. This is normal.

There is also ***abnormal*** anxiety. This is a pathological kind of stress, which if present, is always there. It creates continuous anxiety and often leads to agoraphobia, a word derived from the Greek word meaning "fear of the marketplace or fear of being in public." It is the fear of losing your safe place, the fear of the outside world. One characteristic of anxiety or fear is that it generalizes. Once generalized, it affects one's interaction with friends, relatives, and neighbors—an individual's entire social structure.

Often when around others you simply want to escape to some safe place. Symptoms may include neglecting responsibilities or chores, being unwilling to perform the basic necessities of life, often just wanting to go to bed and stay there all day, doing absolutely nothing.

The conjoined twin of anxiety is depression. Where there is generalized anxiety, there is often accompanying depression. This abnormal anxiety inflates the reality of danger or threat. When the danger appears, you automatically imagine the worst possible result. Rarely does the worst ever actually occur. It is a condition that leads to apprehension and indecision. I'm reminded of Mark Twain who said, "I have dealt with many problems in my life, most of which never existed." That's often how the situation plays out. Twice as many people have generalized anxiety as did in our grandparents' day, possibly because of the incredibly fast-paced world in which we live.

There are several types of anxiety: Generalized anxiety (which we have written about), panic disorders, phobias, post traumatic stress syndrome, social anxiety disorders, separation anxiety, and new ones are being added each year.

One definition of anxiety is stress-induced fear and negative emotions. People, places, and things do not make us feel emotions. We feel emotions because of the way we *think* about people, places, and things. Stress can be both good and bad. Anxiety is sometimes helpful, but often harmful. Helpful stress or anxiety may actually save our lives in critical or dangerous situations. Bad stress or anxiety is being anxious or overly concerned about things over which we have no control. The problem is that our brain does not know the difference between real and imagined threats. We respond the same way emotionally and physically to both real and imagined threats. The most common anxieties are the fear of *lack of control*, the *fear of death*, and the fear of *public speaking*. When we fear a lack of control, even after we know that we have done all we can do in a particular situation, and it is still not enough, then we experience the fear of loss of control. As a result of this, we experience anxiety. We feel powerless, almost overwhelmed. Often, anxiety is also caused by unresolved conflicts. Fears, whether real or imagined, generate the same reaction. Abnormal thought patterns also generate anxiety. This occurs when one learns to think in a negative way. If all thoughts are pessimistic, and one imagines the worst in every situation, then there will be anxiety and fear.

Women are twice as likely to have generalized anxiety than men. In the general population, women seek help for anxiety twice as often as men do. Some deduce it is because women are more in touch with their feelings than men are.

How do we recognize abnormal anxiety? Here are some feelings associated with anxiety:

* A general feeling of uneasiness
* Pacing
* Shaking
* Feeling fatigued
* Increased heart rate
* Increased sweating
* Dry mouth
* Frequent urination
* Muscle tension
* Hyperventilation
* Trouble concentrating
* Poor eating habits
* Rapid speech
* Rapid movement
* Numbness in the hands or face
* Nightmares

* Abdominal pain
* Vomiting
* Pain in the neck and shoulders

All of these can be indications of tension associated with worry and anxiety. Before you diagnose yourself with generalized anxiety, remember that life can be stressful, but that generalized anxiety is seen as abnormal. It concerns stress that is not being dealt with correctly. If you or others close to you feel your anxiety is abnormal, seek professional help.

What are the treatments for anxiety? There is both a medical and a spiritual answer to this question. I believe it takes a combination of the two. We as Christians need to take advantage of the medical accomplishments of our day. If I had been born one hundred years ago, I probably wouldn't have lived to my current age because of my diabetes. Psychotropic drugs are just as legitimate as any other drugs taken for any physical illness. Drugs such as Valium and Xanax work quickly to help relieve anxiety. Take a Xanax and you may feel more relaxed within an hour, even with acute anxiety. Medications are available to help recover from anxiety, but anxiety causes still need to be addressed through therapy. Personally, I don't like prescription drugs for anxiety to be taken on a long-term basis. There are methods like cognitive counseling, which teaches you how to cope with anxiety when it strikes. One thing you can do when feeling an anxiety or panic attack is to add structure—even something so simple as beginning to count slowly from one and continuing to count as high as you need to begin to feel relaxed. Many of the antidepressant drugs will give you hours of relief from anxiety. The difference can literally mean life and death for some people who suffer from generalized anxiety. You need to also do your best to reduce your exposure to whatever makes you anxious. Alcohol and even nicotine can make anxiety worse. There are better drugs than these for relieving stress.

There is also a spiritual treatment. There are things in your life and in mine that are beyond our control. There have been times when I have had to literally drop to my knees and say, "God, I've done all I know to do, and it still isn't enough. I need Your power, Your presence." This is a wonderful benefit of being a Christian, a child of God. We can go to Him with every problem, big or small, real or imagined, and pour it at His feet saying, "Lord, I don't know what to do. I need Your help. I need Your comfort. I need Your healing." In fact, most of the major problems of our lives could be resolved so much quicker and easier if we did what we could and let God take over from there. Do what you can, then give it to God. Beyond what you are capable of doing, the situation should be left in God's hands. He is in control of everything, and He is the One who can help you in all things. This is why I love the passage, "Do not be anxious about anything." That doesn't leave anything out. He says, "Don't be afraid of anything, but with prayer and supplication and thanksgiving...." Wow! Three advantages we have: Prayer. Supplication. Thanksgiving. Get on your knees and pray to God. Tell Him about your fears and doubts. Be earnest. "God, I'm serious about this. I need your help." Offer thanks. When you start counting your blessings, it takes your mind off your problems. So often we go to God and begin to ask for things. We fail to thank Him for what He's already done. We take for granted our clothes, our shelter, our food. We need to take advantage of the fact that we can go to Him and say, "God, I've messed up. I've sinned. I'm wrong. I'm sorry." Guilt no longer becomes an excuse for anxiety because we have the forgiveness of God through Jesus Christ His Son. So why be anxious? We have the Creator on our side. As the saying goes, when you've done all you can, you must let go and let God. The apprehension, the worry, the tension, and the stress disappear. I know that what God is going to do will be what is best for me.

Sometimes I think our problem with anxiety is that we have

too much rather than too little. We have too many things that entangle us in this world. We know this is not our home, but we get distracted. There have been times in my life when things have been taken away from me, and I thought it was the end of the world. I thought I couldn't recover. Time actually does help to heal all wounds, and with time we realize losing things that are unnecessary may bring us the peace we desire.

We must evaluate our lives. We may need to say, "Lord, is there something in my life I need to correct? Show me how can I be better." Job looked at life and realized he wasn't perfect, but he could not find anything deserving of his losing everything. The good news is, when he was at his lowest, he never gave up on God, and God redeemed him. God gave Job twice as much as he had before. Our good portion might not be twice as much as we may have had at one time in our life. But if we let God take control, it certainly takes away the pressure. Wouldn't it be nice to have a pressure valve? We could adjust the pressures in our lives with a quick turn on the nozzle. Thankfully, with God rooting for us, we don't need that valve. And we need to realize that many of the things we think we can't live without may actually be in the way of our getting the most out of life.

> And we know that for those who love God all things work to-gether for good, for those who are called according to his pur-pose. For those whom he foreknew he also predestined to be conformed to the image of his Son, in order that he might be the firstborn among many brothers. And those whom he predestined he also called, and those whom he called he also justified, and those whom he justified he also glorified (Romans 8:28-30, ESV).

We know this passage is talking about Christians, God's chil-dren. We know that for those who love God, all things—no exceptions—work together for good. That means that when we put whatever is causing our worry or anxiety or fear or frustra-tion in God's grace, it comes out for the better. The bitter and the sweet, we are better because of it. If you believe that, your anxieties will lessen.

> What then shall we say to these things? If God is for us, who can be against us? He who did not spare his own Son but gave him up for us all, how will he not also with him graciously give us all things? (Romans 8:31-32, ESV).

God will give us, His children, what we need. Get rid of your preconceived ideas and your prejudices. Don't say, "I won't go to counseling" or "I won't take my medication" or "I won't listen to God's Word." *You* must do everything *you* can. Then you turn the rest over to God. Sometimes we shoot ourselves in the foot with our preconceptions and our pride. Yet when it comes to the preservation of life and health, we need to lose our pride and give what we can to God.

> ...and teaching them to observe all that I have commanded you. And behold, I am with you always, to the end of the age (Matthew 28:20, ESV).

For Christians, our greatest source of comfort comes from our spiritual relationships, the relationship between us and God and between us and our close brothers and sisters in Jesus. Take heart in these verses that show we can be downtrodden but not hopeless:

> "We are afflicted in every way, but not crushed; perplexed, but not driven to despair; persecuted, but not forsaken; struck down, but not destroyed; always carrying in the body the death of Jesus, so that the life of Jesus may also be manifested in our bodies" (2 Corinthians 4:8-10, ESV).

I do not care where I go in this world. God is there. It doesn't matter what country I visit—God is there. It doesn't matter how high on the mountain or deep in the sea I may venture—God is there. All I have to do is speak a whispered word, and it rises to the ear of God. This is faith. Do you believe God is in control? Do you believe God can help you? If you have faith, and you've done what you can, then God will take care of the rest. That's a promise. If you have never put your trust in God after you've done all you can and watched Him work His providence and His care, you can't fathom the extent of God's goodness. God will give you what you need. That does not mean you may not lose some things. It does not mean that the enemies of God's people may not persecute you, but it does mean that God will see you through.

> But you, O LORD, are a shield about me, my glory, and the lifter of my head. I cried aloud to the LORD, and He answered me from his holy hill. I lay down and slept; I woke again, for the LORD sustained me. I will not be afraid of many thousands of people who have set themselves against me all around (Psalm 3:3-6, ESV).

I pray every night, "God, put your shield of protection around my family, friends, and loved ones." God is our shield. God through our faith is the One who helps repel the fiery darts of the evil one.

When you read Matthew and Luke and see how many times God says, "Do not be afraid," it is amazing. When the world is looking at us saying, "You can't believe that," and "You can't do that," God tells us, "Don't be afraid. Stand for what is right, and don't be afraid."

There are two laws we live by: the law of the world, which says, you get what you can get from anybody by any means. Lie, steal, cheat—whatever you have to do to get what you want, then that's what you must do. It may be a pragmatic *view* of life, but it is a destructive *way* of life. The spiritual law says, "God, I'm going to do what is right no matter what the consequences. If You take away my home or I lose my health, my money, or even my life, it will not dissuade me from living the way You want me to live. I will still be honest, righteous, and godly. I will still be Your servant." You cannot live by both standards. You can't straddle the fence, because that will often make you more anxious, frustrated, depressed, and even angry. It is not easy to live God's way. When someone comes at you with all the power of government or powerful evil people, it is difficult to say, "I'm going to stand my ground and stand by God and for God."

> My flesh and my heart may fail, but God is the strength of my heart and my portion forever. For behold, those who are far from you shall perish; you put an end to everyone who is unfaithful to you. But for me it is good to be near God; I have made the LORD God my refuge, that I may tell of all your works (Psalm 73:26-28, ESV).

> …praying at all times in the Spirit, with all prayer and supplication. To that end, keep alert with all perseverance, making supplication for all the saints… (Ephesians 6:18, ESV).

As God's fellowship, His people, we must help one another. When we have a problem, we share our faith and try to help. We do not live in constant anxiety because perfect love truly does cast out fear.

> Then they cried to the LORD in their trouble, and he delivered them from their distress. He brought them out of darkness and the shadow of death, and burst their bonds apart (Psalm 107:13,14, ESV).

Questions

1. What is the definition of anxiety?
2. Approximately how many Americans suffer from anxiety each year?
3. Why is a good physical checkup necessary when feeling anxiety?
4. Why is sleep so important in dealing with anxiety and depression?
5. Is anxiety normal? What would be an example of "good" anxiety?

6. What is abnormal anxiety?

7. What is the "conjoined twin" of anxiety?

8. Do you believe we have more anxiety today than in our grandparents' day?

9. What do you think are the most common fears that cause anxiety? Of what are you most afraid?

10. What are some of the symptoms associated with abnormal anxiety?

11. What are the two primary methods of treating anxiety today?

12. What are some of the spiritual advantages Christians have in overcoming anxiety?

13. Read Romans 8:31-32 and discuss how it relates to helping with anxiety.

14. Read through Matthew and Luke and see how many times God says "Do not be afraid," "Do not be anxious," or "Do not worry."

CHAPTER 4

PAUL'S PROBLEM
WITH DEPRESSION

B lessed be the God and Father of our Lord Jesus Christ, the
Father of mercies and God of all comfort, who comforts us
in all our affliction, so that we may be able to comfort those who
are in any affliction, with the comfort with which we ourselves
are comforted by God. For as we share abundantly in Christ's
sufferings, so through Christ we share abundantly in comfort
too. If we are afflicted, it is for your comfort and salvation; and
if we are comforted, it is for your comfort, which you experience
when you patiently endure the same sufferings that we suffer.
Our hope for you is unshaken, for we know that as you share in
our sufferings, you will also share in our comfort.

For we do not want you to be unaware, brothers, of the affliction we experienced in Asia. For we were so utterly burdened
beyond our strength that we despaired of life itself. Indeed, we
felt that we had received the sentence of death. But that was to
make us rely not on ourselves but on God who raises the dead.
He delivered us from such a deadly peril, and he will deliver us.
On him we have set our hope that he will deliver us again. You
also must help us by prayer, so that many will give thanks on
our behalf for the blessing granted us through the prayers of
many (2 Corinthians 1:3-11, ESV).

During the time he wrote this letter to the church at Ephesus,
Paul was experiencing difficulty and distress because of his situation. The difficulty had to do with his ministry and the many
problems associated with being an apostle and living up to the
high expectations people of that day had for apostles. He was a
preacher of the gospel, delivering a message that an evil world

did not want to hear. The word he uses in the Greek is *thlipsis*, which means "to live in distress or to carry an emotional burden; to be emotionally upset." And he had good reason to be distressed! On his first trip to Corinth he had just left Athens and, as he traveled the forty miles between Athens and Corinth, he reflected on the harsh and difficult times he had experienced: debating with the philosophers and educators of Athens and making little progress toward teaching them about Jesus. As he traveled toward Corinth, he determined to know nothing among the Corinthians except "Jesus Christ and him crucified" (1 Corinthians 2:2, ESV). He would no longer be concerned with the false philosophies and ideals of the world of his day. In his second letter to the Corinthians, Paul wanted them to know of the problems he had suffered in the name of Jesus. He shared his difficult, even bad, experiences so the Corinthians could help in his consolation and know where their consolation came from when they experienced difficult times. God through Jesus was Paul's ultimate consolation. It is essential for us to help one another and "bear each other's burdens" as we live together in the world. Paul gives praise and honor and glory to God. He has come to more fully understand the God of Abraham, Isaac, and Jacob—the God of Moses—the God of the Old Testament and the Father of Jesus Christ, our Lord and Savior.

Paul Needs Comforting

Paul needed to be comforted because of the suffering he had experienced for Jesus. Jesus lived, preached, and healed. Despite all the good He did, He was rejected by evil people, nailed to a cruel cross, suffered, and died. As a follower of Jesus, Paul suspected that this might be the end result of his life, too. His world was an evil one, full of sin, as is ours. Listen to any newscast, read any newspaper, associate with any cosmopolitan group, and you will see that evil is very much alive and well today. God's people have always suffered because of the evil rejection of God and His principles. Paul identified with Jesus' suffering. He was a messenger, an ambassador of Christ. He was a chosen apostle, to whom Jesus was revealed after His death, burial, resurrection, and ascension. Living for Jesus had brought Paul pain, incredible opposition, and rejection by the very people he came to help, just as it did for his Lord. This is why Paul was experiencing some emotional problems—why he was somewhat depressed. Satan continues even today to spread his evil—do you doubt sin, evil, and the devil's influence? Evil has been written on every page of history and continues to plague God's people today. God wanted His people to live in peace, with Him and with one another. It wasn't that way in Corinth, though, just as it has never been that way anywhere since man's fall. As God's people, we are today a community of suffering pilgrims. If one of us suffers, we all suffer, and we each must comfort one another.

Tony Meyer, author and lecturer, in an article entitled *"Life for a Dark Path,"* chronicled how many of God's people are hurting, suffering, misunderstood, even rejected, and are receiving little or no comfort even from the fellowship of believers. "I think there are many reasons why this is true. Because of the stigma associated with mental illness it does require a great deal of effort and understanding to help those who are depressed or anxious or who have any one of a number of emotional or mental illnesses. No one Christian can give the comfort needed by his or her self; it takes a fellowship of Christian believers to be effective in helping those who are in distress. Many Christians are filled with depression and anxiety, not knowing which way to turn, looking for support. When friends are struck down by physical disability, we are sympathetic and understanding; we visit them, cook meals, send cards, and call. But when a brother or sister becomes disabled with Alzheimer's, or neurosis, or is admitted to a psychiatric hospital, there's a big question as to what we as God's people can do. How can we help? Will what we do help or hurt? Often, we do nothing. However, just as people in the church become physically sick, they also get emotionally and mentally sick, and as Paul encourages compassion and comfort (2 Corinthians 1:3-6), we must be willing to step out in faith and be there for all of God's hurting people."

Prepare yourself and watch what you say to those who are hurting. Often we go to someone with platitudes or meaningless, hurtful sayings such as, "Man up," "Just get over it," "Don't worry"—all of which mean nothing but more pain to a person who is barely hanging on to sanity.

Cindy Holtrop, author of the blog *Pathways to Promise—Putting Faith in Mental Health Recovery*, writes about her experience with depression. She says, "Throughout my life I have experienced bouts of depression. I have said darkness is my closest friend (reference to Psalms 88). The most recent depression lasted three years and took another year for me to recover. I felt abandoned by God, isolated without hope, and without any sense of the future. I wondered if I would ever get well." Here's advice she gives to anyone trying to comfort those with mental illness: "First, just listen. Let people who are suffering in this way tell their story. Most of us have not walked in their shoes, or we have not experienced mental illness, we have not had their experience. Listen with elephant ears to what they have to say. Second, accept them where they are. We should not bring more judgment on the depressed. They are already feeling terrible enough and are struggling to stay in touch with God. Many people in the grip of mental illness feel abandoned by God—darkness is their closest friend; this is why acceptance by others, love, and encouragement can be the best medicine. A person with a mental illness is not just the illness. They have many gifts and strengths. Third, pray for those who are suffering. Sometimes the suffering person does not feel he can pray. It helps to have others praying for them—a card, an encouraging note, a phone call, a prayer all can be used by God to bring comfort to someone who is struggling."

The Psalms can be especially helpful; Psalm 30 gives voice to deep despair but also to trust in God.

> I will extol you, O LORD, for you have drawn me up
>   and have not let my foes rejoice over me.
> O LORD my God, I cried to you for help,
>   and you have healed me.
> O LORD, you have brought up my soul from Sheol;
>   you restored me to life from among those who go down
>   to the pit.
> Sing praises to the LORD, O you his saints,
>   and give thanks to his holy name.
> For his anger is but for a moment,
>   and his favor is for a lifetime.
> Weeping may tarry for the night,
>   but joy comes with the morning.
> As for me, I said in my prosperity,
>   "I shall never be moved."
> By your favor, O LORD,
>   you made my mountain stand strong;
> you hid your face;
>   I was dismayed.
> To you, O LORD, I cry,
>   and to the LORD I plead for mercy:
> "What profit is there in my death,
>   if I go down to the pit?
> Will the dust praise you?
>   Will it tell of your faithfulness?
> Hear, O LORD, and be merciful to me!
>   O LORD, be my helper!"
> You have turned for me my mourning into dancing;
>   you have loosed my sackcloth
>   and clothed me with gladness,
> that my glory may sing your praise and not be silent.
>   O LORD my God, I will give thanks to you forever!

When someone is struggling to believe, sometimes the community around them has to believe for them and in them, we have to carry them along in faith until the darkness lifts and their fear subsides. Many chronically mentally ill people lose contact with friends and family over time. When an illness does not heal quickly people get tired, they get worn out, they lose their friends—that is why the Christian community has to practice endurance and perseverance. This is why we do the hard work of being the church and being the community of Christ. The church is God's hospital.

Mental and emotional illnesses are complex and not easy to treat. There is much that we still do not understand. You cannot diagnose a mental illness with a blood test, an X-ray, or a CT scan. They are not easy to treat because there are no quick resolutions. Treatment and recovery come only after time and effort, with many ups and downs and much patience.

We live in a day of quick fixes, instant gratification, and we have little patience with anything we do not understand or like. In God's providence, He has given us tools to cope until we recover, and the patience and grace to bear with our thorn in the flesh.

The first tool is *time*. Often we are simply too impatient, expecting instant miracles, when the lesson we may need to learn is patience and understanding. The old adage that "time heals all wounds" has a definite element of truth. It may not be true of all wounds, but it certainly helps to lessen the pain, which we could never bear if that pain were as fresh as when it first happened. Be patient with yourself, be patient with others, and be patient with God, because somehow in God's crucible He is mixing all the events of your life together. With the pestle of your experience and with His mercy and grace, and the comfort and help from God's people, we endure, get past, and get through our difficult times in life and heal.

What then shall we say to these things? If God is for us, who can be against us? He who did not spare his own Son but gave him up for us all, how will he not also with him graciously give us all things? Who shall bring any charge against God's elect? It is God who justifies. Who is to condemn? Christ Jesus is the one who died—more than that, who was raised—who is at the right hand of God, who indeed is interceding for us. Who shall separate us from the love of Christ? Shall tribulation, or distress, or persecution, or famine, or nakedness, or danger, or sword? As it is written, "For your sake we are being killed all the day long; we are regarded as sheep to be slaughtered." No, in all these things we are more than conquerors through him who loved us. For I am sure that neither death nor life, nor angels nor rulers, nor things present nor things to come, nor powers, nor height nor depth, nor anything else in all creation, will be able to separate us from the love of God in Christ Jesus our Lord (Romans 8:31-39, ESV).

As for you, always be sober-minded, endure suffering, do the work of an evangelist, fulfill your ministry.

For I am already being poured out as a drink offering, and the time of my departure has come. I have fought the good fight, I have finished the race, I have kept the faith. Henceforth there is laid up for me the crown of righteousness, which the Lord, the righteous judge, will award to me on that day, and not only to me but also to all who have loved his appearing (2 Timothy 4:5-8, ESV).

What We Understand Today About Depression

Many factors are involved in depression. We have more than one hundred billion neurons in our brains and more than one hundred trillion synapses, not to mention innumerable brain cells. Various parts of the brain utilize the electro-chemical transmission parts of the brain to assist in thinking and feeling. The cells that do the work of the brain are neurons. These neurons process, send, and receive messages, enabling the brain to perceive the world, carry out all intentional actions, think, problem solve, form and retrieve memory, and generate emotions and mood. There are others cells in the brain called glia. It is possible the brain may have more glia cells than neurons. The glia cells provide essential support to neurons and act as the brain's immune system, since the brain is largely cut off from the body's regular immune system by blood-brain barriers. Brain chemicals are acetylcholine, norepinephrine, dopamine, serotonin, Gamma-amino butyric acid, glutamate, and endorphins. Each of these chemicals has a specific purpose in the brain, and any imbalances result in specific disturbances of the brain. As an example, low levels of serotonin, norephinephrine, and dopamine are thought to be involved in depression. Many of the drugs on the market today to help with depression are targeted at increasing the levels of serotonin, norepinephrine, and dopamine. There are certainly other factors, such as the level of glutamates and neurotrophic factors.

Dysthymia is a condition in which the adult is depressed for at least two years. If it is chronic, it can last as long as five years. Depression makes it difficult, if not impossible, for a person to carry out daily responsibilities.

Subtypes of Depression

* Premenstrual dysphonic disorder.
* Antepartum or repartee depression.
* Postpartum or after-birth depression. Surprisingly, 10 percent of fathers actually experience a kind of postpartum depression.
* Psychotic depression.
* Seasonal affective disorder (SAD), usually associated with a lack of sunlight.
* Substance-induced depression.
* Grief depression.

Anhendonia is a condition characterized by a loss of interest in things that once were pleasurable. What do you do for fun?

When was the last time you did what you enjoyed? When we stop enjoying the legitimate pleasures of life, we are headed in the direction of depression.

Questions

1. Discuss 2 Corinthians 1:3-11. Why was Paul experiencing difficulty and distress?

2. Why do you think Paul needed comforting?

3. Discuss the trials and tribulations Paul had experienced as an apostle.

4. Do we treat people with physical illnesses differently than those with mental or emotional problems?

5. Read and comment on Psalm 30 and how it relates to depression as well as hope and trust in God.

6. What are some tools to recovering from depression?

7. Discuss how marvelously the brain is developed by God— the incredible number of synapses and brain cells as well as the electro-chemical transmitters and the neurons involved, that help us to think, problem solve, retrieve memories, and generate emotion and mood.

8. What are some subtypes of depression?

9. What is anhendonia?

10. Have you experienced depression? (optional)

CHAPTER 5

GRIEF:
THE NIGHT BEFORE CHRISTMAS

Biblical Example

Mary, Martha, and Lazarus were close friends of Jesus. In fact, we read in John 11:5, "Now Jesus loved Martha and her sister and Lazarus." They were close, and Mary and Martha believed that Jesus would do whatever possible to help them in their hour of need. Jesus received word that Lazarus was deathly ill, and that the sisters were hoping He could come immediately. But to everyone's surprise, Jesus delayed His trip and stayed where He was for two more days. Jesus was aware that Lazarus had already died, and He delayed His coming to Mary and Martha so that He could show His power over death. "Lazarus has died, and for your sake, I am glad that I was not there, so that you may believe. But let us go to Him" (John 11:14,15). When Jesus arrived, He found that Lazarus had already been in the tomb four days, and many friends had come to console Mary and Martha. "When Martha heard that Jesus was coming, she went and met Him, but Mary remained seated in the house. Martha said to Jesus, 'Lord, if you had been here, my brother would not have died. But even now I know that whatever you ask from God, God will give you.' Jesus said to her, 'Your brother will rise again'" (John 11:20-23, ESV). At this time, Jesus performs one of His greatest miracles—foretelling His own death and resurrection as well as the resurrection of the faithful to God. As He had power to raise Lazarus from the dead, so He has power over all death, and someday we will be resurrected to spend eternity with Him.

Grief comes to all of us, including our Savior, in one way or another and at one time or another. "Jesus wept" (John 11:35). But because of the consolation and comfort Jesus gave to Mary and Martha, in the resurrection of Lazarus, and His conquering death with His own resurrection and ascension, Jesus gives us hope in the face of grief.

In my family, all of my siblings (three sisters) scattered to other areas, away from my hometown of North Little Rock, Arkansas. One sister lived in Atlanta; I was living in Nashville, Tennessee; and another resided in a distant part of Arkansas. Our youngest sister had been suffering from a chronic debilitating progressive disease for some time. On Christmas morning a few years ago, she was rushed to the hospital and passed away later that day. Christmas has never really been the same, especially for my mother and father, but also for my two surviving sisters and me. A day celebrated as being happy and full of hope had ended in my sister's death—at age 37. There was lots of sadness and sorrowing, many questions without immediate answers, and even a little guilt spread about here and there for not having been with her more often during her illness.

The death of a loved one evokes some of the most powerful emotions we have. More recently, my parents, aunts and uncles, and even cousins have passed. They were much older—in fact, some had lived to their mid-90s. Although there was a distinct sense of loss, there was also the realization of the cycle of life. When a person is taken prematurely, especially a child, all emotions are intensified. The reality is that all of us experience grief during our lifetime. If we live long enough, we may suffer numerous episodes of grief. It is important that we understand the grieving process and that we successfully deal with the realities of our loss. Those losses need not be a life. They can be the loss of a relationship through separation or divorce, the loss of a job, a close friendship, or a close pet companion. Losses come in all shapes, sizes, and colors. But each of them has similar character-istics and similar stages of acceptance and reconciliation.

Some Counterproductive Actions and Reactions

I don't know why it is at the time of loss that one of the first emotions to surface is that of blame or guilt. No one always does everything they should or could in any relationship. As human beings we make mistakes, say things we regret, do things we should not, and often neglect those we love. The only possible purpose of guilt and blame is to allow it to correct whatever per-ceived shortcomings we may have. We know we can receive the forgiveness of God, and we also understand that if we are sincerely sorry, apologize, and ask for forgiveness, we can normally receive that from friends and loved ones. But to carry the burden of guilt and blame long term is harmful and debilitating physically, men-tally, and spiritually.

I have often wondered why we have to have a reason or assign blame every time there is a tragedy. Sometimes, things just hap-pen. There is no rhyme or reason and no blame to be assessed. There are some whose personality is such that unless they can find a reason to blame, they cannot feel complete about a loss. That often unnecessarily further alienates and causes hurt to others. Those who spend a lifetime playing the judging game are most often unhappy and incomplete, and they are unable to resolve the grief and sorrow that may come their way. Sometimes we just have to accept the reality of the loss and let go of the blame. Jesus said "Judge not, that you be not judged. For with the judgment you pronounce you will be judged, and with the measure you use it will be measured to you" (Matthew 7:1-2, ESV). We do not know others' hearts as God does. We don't understand all the circumstances of loss and tragedy as God does. So we must leave the judgment and the blame to His discretion. Forgiveness is one of the essential elements of getting past grief and loss. Jesus said that if we are unwilling to forgive others, we will not be forgiven.

Forgiveness is cyclic. God through Jesus forgives us; we forgive each other; and God forgives us again.

When there is a loss involving a Christian or a child, we can go to God's Word for special encouragement and strength:

> But we do not want you to be uninformed, brothers, about those who are asleep, that you may not grieve as others do who have no hope. For since we believe that Jesus died and rose again, even so, through Jesus, God will bring with him those who have fallen asleep. For this we declare to you by a word from the Lord, that we who are alive, who are left until the coming of the Lord, will not precede those who have fallen asleep. For the Lord himself will descend from heaven with a cry of command, with the voice of an archangel, and with the sound of the trumpet of God. And the dead in Christ will rise first. Then we who are alive, who are left, will be caught up together with them in the clouds to meet the Lord in the air, and so we will always be with the Lord. Therefore encourage one another with these words (1 Thessalonians 4:13-18, ESV).

Paul is writing to a bereaved church. He has only been away six months, but during that time, there have been several who have passed away, and these brothers and sisters are mourning their loss. They write to Paul, asking "What is the attitude we should have toward those who have died in the Lord?" In response, Paul uses a word that is exclusively Christian. The word in the Greek is *koimeterion*, which means "a sleeping place or a place of rest." The world that does not believe in the resurrection calls it a graveyard, but when Jesus came and conquered death, Christians referred to the resting place of the body as a sleeping place. We have a similar word in our own English language. It is comparable to the Greek word, except we pronounce it in English "cemetery" or "place of sleep."

At the time of loss, our emotions are intensified. They may even be said to be "raw" or "on edge." Our grief is real and often uncontrolled. I think of David's sorrow at the death of his son,

Absalom. It is recorded in 2 Samuel 18:33. "And the king was deeply moved and went up to the chamber over the gate and wept. And as he went, he said, 'O my son Absalom, my son, my son Absalom! Would I had died instead of you, O Absalom, my son, my son!'" (ESV). David's sad cry is the cry of every grieving parent who unexpectedly loses a child. Often in the midst of such immediate sorrow we say and do things that are irrational, even bizarre. We should not, however, blame ourselves. There will be time later for apologies and seeking forgiveness for hurtful words.

The Five Stages of Grief and Loss

The feelings of grief and loss are so universal and historical that they can be categorized, identified, and named. Over many years psychiatrists, psychologists, and psychotherapists have observed the similarity of reactions in time of great loss and have come to describe these as the five stages of grief and loss. They were first listed together by psychiatrist Elisabeth Kubler-Ross in 1969. We do not go through each of these states all at once, and we will possibly get stuck in one of them longer than others. But anyone who has ever experienced devastating loss can identify with the reality of these stages. Many people will not experience each of these stages in the order we will discuss them, and for some the transition from one stage to another may be so quick as to not be recognizable. Each of us grieves differently. Some will be vocal and emotional in their grieving, while others will internalize their grief and may cry very little. We should never judge the degree of a person's grief by outward appearance.

Denial—The First Stage of Grief

Denial and isolation are usually the first reactions to a significant loss. I remember my first experience with denial. I had only been in practice a few months when I received a call from a friend who is the director of a funeral home. He asked if I would try to console grieving parents who had just lost their ten-year-old son. When I arrived, the mother was on the floor, pounding her fists and crying, "I don't want any of the coffins! I don't want him placed in any of them!" Her story was tragic. She had been told she would never be able to have children, but she did give birth to the one son. He was an ideal child and brought them great pleasure. On his tenth birthday he received a bicycle. He was riding it down the sidewalk when suddenly he lost control, fell, hit his head on the pavement, and died instantly. Any parent can identify with the horror and pain those parents were feeling. It took several years of intense therapy before the mother came to grips with the full reality of the loss of her son.

There are losses from which we never fully, completely recover. I had a good friend several years ago who was extremely close to his wife. They had never had children, and he treated his wife literally as a queen. She died unexpectedly, and her untimely death was a tragedy from which he never fully recovered. Each day after her burial, he would go to the cemetery and sit in a lawn chair for hours, talking to the grave. This ritual went on for over two years, at which time he died, in my judgment, from a broken heart and a grieving spirit. There are realities in our lives that are so devastating to us that we cannot fully accept them immediately, and sometimes we can never accept them well enough to go on living a complete life.

I had a patient whose husband died at home in the night. She found him the next morning. She went to her neighbor and said, "Something is wrong with my husband. I can't wake him up." The neighbor went back with her and, sure enough, he had died in his sleep. The woman never accepted the death of her husband. Whenever anyone visited she would say, "He must be hunting or fishing. I'm expecting him home any time." Or she would say, "He's gone to visit relatives," or offer another excuse for his not being present. This complete denial went on for several years until her death.

It is essential that we not get stuck in any one of the stages of grief. But it is especially important that we accept the reality of the loss so that we may move on to complete the other steps necessary to accomplish acceptance. Isolation is sometimes a lesser form of denial in which we may intellectually have understood the loss but we isolate ourselves from other people so that we don't have to discuss the loss or to minimize the memories of the loss. It is vitally important that we have those closest to us with us as quickly as possible to help in the grieving process. This helps us to understand and accept the reality of the loss.

Anger—The Second Stage of Grief

The second stage of grieving is usually anger. As reality sets in and the isolation begins to diminish, the emotional pain becomes excessive. The intense emotions of full realization of the loss cause us to experience the pain more acutely. Usually our anger is generalized, where we just feel angry at everything, everyone, every feeling, and often even God. We know that those close to us were not to blame for the loss, but somehow we want to blame. Anger is a way of expressing of that feeling. We may even be angry with the person who died because, in our mind, that person caused the pain by dying or leaving. Sometimes we say hurtful things in that anger, even hurtful things to and about God. But as we begin to heal, there will be time to ask for the forgiveness of friends, relatives, and God and be assured that all who care about us, as God does, will grant that forgiveness. I have known people to blame health care professionals, but it is a useless exercise in futility to place blame and may only hinder the healing process.

Bargaining—The Third Stage of Grief

Bargaining, or rationalization, is a means of trying to regain some control and understanding of what has happened. As an ill loved one nears death, we may begin to try to bargain for his or her life. "Please God, spare my loved one, and I promise I will spend the rest of my life serving You." Guilt is often a part of this process. The "if only" and "why me" statements cause us to find fault not only with ourselves, but also with others. We all experience situations that are beyond our control and, yes, it is perfectly normal to do everything we possibly can to prolong life or a relationship, but the reality is, we are all terminal. At some point we will die. At some time or in some way, relationships will be broken. When we realize that death is imminent, we may begin a possibly legitimate kind of bargaining, hoping that the death will be painless and that the life lived will be an inspiration to those remaining. We can look forward to reuniting with our loved ones in heaven. "What ifs" or "if only" or "I should haves" serve little purpose in accepting the tragic reality that our loved on has passed or that a relationship has ended.

Depression—The Fourth Stage of Grief

Some elements of depression are normal when we experience a significant loss. We are sad. We have regrets. And then there are realities that set in about how we are going to manage financially and how the one left behind can manage all the chores and tasks that it previously took two to complete. Depression is sometimes defined as "anger turned inward," and we need to get through the anger stage as quickly and effectively as possible. In doing so, we will lessen the depressive feelings related to our loss.

It is acceptable to take antidepressants and/or anti-anxiety medication short term during great tragedies and losses. Some may feel it is a sign of moral weakness and, for some, it isn't necessary. But one should not feel guilty for taking such medications for a short time to help them cope with the immediate loss. If one successfully passes through each of the grieving stages, he will find himself less and less in need of medication.

Acceptance—The Fifth Stage of Grief

There are degrees of acceptance. Some losses are so great that we will never be able to get completely over them. But we can come to the point of accepting the reality and moving on with our day-to-day responsibilities and obligations as well as being able to reunite socially with our friends, relatives, and loved ones. As the anniversary of the loss approaches each year, a person might find himself drifting back to one or more of the stages of grief and loss, if only for a few days. One way to minimize this is to remember all the good qualities, good times, and good memories instead of dwelling on the negative on these anniversaries.

There is no timetable for the grieving process. Some will take longer on one or other of the stages. Some will go through the stages so quickly that it is difficult to identify them. Environmental circumstances, the amount of support available, and even one's personal faith can all affect the timetable, but the secret is to progress at your own pace, taking care not to get stuck in one of the phases longer than is healthy but to move on toward peace and acceptance.

Hopeful, Helpful Suggestions

It is impossible to give a "one size fits all" recommendation for overcoming grief, but there are certain things we can do that may help us in returning to some sense of normalcy.

(1) Stay busy. Work is therapeutic. Work gives us a sense of purpose and value.

(2) Experience catharsis. Don't be afraid to talk about the loss. As a matter of fact, if you have trusted friends or a good therapist, talking about it can be an effective release of emotion.

(3) Allow yourself to cry. Crying is nature's emotional release. It helps rid us of the emotional toxins that build up in our body and spirit.

(4) Pray. Pray regularly and often for strength, encouragement, and for the ability and opportunity to continue doing well.

Realize that time helps heal, but does not completely heal, all wounds. It's only natural and normal to occasionally feel the pain of a loss. Some people have confided in me that there are moments even years after a great loss when they are overwhelmed with the same intense pain as at the original time of loss. This phenomenon usually lasts only a short time, but is a reminder that our memories are powerful emotional stimulants.

(5) Invest as much of your time as you can in helping others. There were many people who may have comforted you in your time of loss, and certainly God was there to help you through it. By passing it on, it gives one a feeling of accomplishment and purpose.

(6) Don't feel guilty about feeling relieved. Often when there has been a prolonged illness, or much pain associated with the dying process, the survivor has a feeling of relief, a sense of completeness when the loved one passes. This feeling of relief is a normal feeling for a person who has experienced prolonged observation of a loved one going through pain, suffering, and sorrow. It is acceptable and understandable.

All of us experience losses of various kinds. There is the problem of personal suffering or the suffering of a loved one. The problems associated with aging are unique to themselves. The loss of a significant other, dealing with broken homes, even problems such as the empty nest—all have their challenges. But as we go through these various difficulties and problems, we need to learn the coping skills necessary to successfully and adequately heal from each stage of life and each tragedy we experience.

Questions

1. What are some kinds of loss that can create grief?

2. What are some counterproductive actions to grief as a result of some loss?

3. At the time of death or loss, why do we feel the need to blame someone or something?

4. How does forgiveness play into overcoming grief?

5. Read 1 Thessalonians 4:13-18 and discuss how this helps in our ability to deal with death.

6. What are the five stages of grief?

7. Discuss each of the various stages of grief.

8. What happens if we get stuck in one of these stages for a prolonged period of time?

9. Is anyone exempt from grief?

10. How long should we follow up with those who have experienced great loss through death, illness, or other tragedies? Is it enough just to be there at the beginning of the loss?

CHAPTER 6

BIPOLAR AND OBSESSIVE COMPUSIVE DISORDERS

Biblical Example

Sometimes we become so confused in our thinking that we develop destructive thought patterns. Such was the case of King Saul in his relationship with David. It was a gradual process that led him to his obsessions. One need not have the neurological diagnosis of obsessive-compulsive disorder to give in to obsessive or compulsive behavior. Saul became jealous and envious of the attention David gained after killing Goliath as well as the reception David received from the people of Israel. Saul began to obsess on every victory of David's and sought in his obsessive mindset to kill David. This created many problems for Saul's kingdom and for his relationship with his son, Jonathan. Obsessive and compulsive behavior often leads us to extremely irrational behavior and almost always ends badly.

Another example of obsessive or compulsive behavior, though with less harmful consequences, would be that of Mary and Martha:

> "Now as they went on their way, Jesus entered a village. And a woman named Martha welcomed him into her house. And she had a sister called Mary, who sat at the Lord's feet and listened to his teaching. But Martha was distracted with much serving. And she went up to him and said, 'Lord, do you not care that my sister has left me to serve alone? Tell her then to help me!' But the Lord answered her, 'Martha, Martha, you are anxious and troubled about many things. But one thing is necessary. Mary has chosen the good portion, which will not be taken away from her'" (Luke 10:38-42, ESV).

Sometimes we become so obsessed with the little things in life, such as keeping the house spotless, working endless hours at our job, pursuing our hobbies to the point of obsession, or compulsively devoting ourselves to less than worthwhile goals, that we neglect the more important matters of life. We can literally become obsessed with almost anything. When one examines the lives of biblical characters, it becomes obvious that those who were most often used by the Lord were not perfect, but had a good heart. Such biblical characters as Abraham, Isaac, Jacob, Noah, Moses, David, Ruth, Peter, Paul, John, Luke, Timothy, and many others all had similarities. They were not perfect. Many of them made mistakes. But their heart was such that they repented and corrected those mistakes. On occasion certain of these biblical characters may have briefly experienced what could be diagnosed as a mental or emotional problem. As we go through each chapter in this book, we will realize that good mental and emotional health is a wonderful asset in living a happy, useful, and productive life.

One does not have to be clinically diagnosed as having an obsessive-compulsive disorder to exhibit obsessive and compulsive attitudes and dispositions. Whenever we fixate on one thing, one person, or one situation and cannot think or consider any other issue, we are being obsessive and/or compulsive. Over the years in my practice, I have seen individuals obsess on another person, to the extent that they try to control that person's entire life. Jealousy is involved—wanting to know where they are, what they are doing and why, and even objecting to certain behaviors or associations with other people. This kind of possessive obsession-compulsion is always destructive and often leads to violence. Any time a relationship becomes abnormally possessive, obsessive, or compulsive, it is a toxic relationship and one that should be either ended or the obsessive-compulsive person must seek therapy and make conscious changes to their thoughts.

It was this kind of relationship that Saul had with David. His compulsive behavior led to a bad ending for Saul. No matter what the motivation for the obsessive-compulsive behavior may be [whether it is an intellectual disagreement, a religious conflict, or a matter or selfishness, jealousy, or pride] obsessions, compulsions, and addictions almost always lead to disastrous consequences.

Bipolar Disorder

Kay Redfield Jamison, Ph. D., is a psychologist with bipolar disorder. In an article entitled "A Unique Mind," she says, "Manic depressive disorder, mood, and thoughts incite dreadful behavior, destroy the basis of rational thought, and too often erode the desire and will to live. It is an illness that is biological in origin, yet one feels psychologically the experience of it. An illness that is unique in conferring advantage and pleasure, yet one that brings in its wake almost unendurable suffering and not infrequent suicide… I am fortunate that I have not died from my illness, fortunate in having received the best medical care available, and fortunate in having friends, colleagues, and family who support me."

Bipolar disorder is divided into several categories. There is major bipolar disorder, as well as bipolar I and bipolar II disorder. It takes a trained professional to note the differences in the bipolar condition and to understand the subtle differences to proper treatment.

Facts about bipolar disorder:

* Bipolar disorder is a treatable disorder, but unlike major depression, may not be curable in most people.

* Bipolar disorder usually begins in late adolescence or early adulthood and occurs equally among men and women.

* Most people with bipolar disorder will cycle only once a year or so with episodes lasting three to six months. In some people, there can be long periods of remission, even months or years with no major symptoms.

* Bipolar disorder nearly always must be treated with medication, although psychotherapy and behavior therapy are necessary for remission in most patients. Some patients can be treated with mood stabilizing medications for manic episodes. Some doctors will add antipsychotic and anti-depressive medications.

* A major problem in treating non-compliant patients is when a person is in a manic state they feel too well to comply with the continuance of their medication, often saying, "I feel better than I ever have. I don't need to take my medication any longer."

* The exact cause of bipolar disorder is unknown, but involves epigenetic changes, altered brain neurochemistry and structure, dietary factors, medical disorders, obesity, environmental triggers, and other medical disorders. All of these may be involved. A proper diagnosis may be life saving, because when a person is properly treated, he or she usually responds positively.

There is another class of patients usually classified in the major depressive area with a family history of bipolar disorder that is often referred to as bipolar III. These patients tend to exhibit subtle hypomanic tendencies (hypomanic means a lower level of mania) and are often achievement-oriented and driven individuals.

Source: James Coggin, MD, Merikangas, et al.

Symptoms of Mania:
* An inflated sense of one's own ability, which often causes a person to be accident prone.

* Speaking very fast because the brain is racing and thoughts are coming so quickly that speech cannot keep up with the rapid brain activity.

* Jumping from one idea to another, very easily distracted.
* Changing subjects quickly.

Bipolar is one disorder as far as we know that cannot be cured, but it can be controlled. It may be a hereditary problem. Certain chemicals are essential to brain function: serotonin, dopamine, norepinephrine, glutamates, ZABA. These help electromagnetic impulses that send messages from the brain to the body. A bipolar individual may have an imbalance in one or more of these areas. One goal is to try to balance the brain's chemistry to improve mood. People who have bipolar disorder are three times more likely to have a depressive state than a manic phase. They may have a brief period of stabilization, then depression, stabilization, depression, then mania. And the pattern continues.

Many bipolar patients can make you think the decisions they are making are perfectly normal and rational even though, as you listen to their explanation as a therapist, you know it is a disastrous decision. They usually have good reasons for spending too much money, gambling, taking risks with business ventures, or participating in risky sexual encounters, and they often believe they have supernatural abilities or talents. I had a patient tell me recently that I may have a doctorate, but that they were much smarter than I because they were street savvy and had special intuitive abilities to read people's minds. This person, in the manic stage of bipolar disorder, shared that on the way to her appointment she had raced with someone at speeds reaching over 100 miles an hour in a neighborhood area and felt that it was not an unsafe activity.

The depressive phase of bipolar disorder is a dark, bleak place, as with most depression. It is a place that people have described to me as being "the worst feeling I have ever had." Others have said, "This is the most pain I have ever experienced." Still others, "I have never experienced any physical pain to compare with my depressive pain." It is often described as being one of the most hopeless feelings a person can experience. Once on medication and therapy, patients note a clear improvement. The person begins to stabilize, and attitude improves.

Often people with bipolar disorder need someone to monitor their medication. I spoke with someone recently who has a relative with bipolar disorder. That individual has a caretaker to assure the patient takes the medication as prescribed. Even the government in some instances recognizes the need for a medicine caretaker for bipolar patients.

Bipolar patients are often given SSRI drugs (selective serotonin reuptake inhibitors). These drugs attempt to balance the serotonin in the brain. Bipolar patients may also be given antipsychotic and mood elevating drugs as well as anti depressants. When there is an effective combination of medications and they are taken regularly, the patient's mood begins to stabilize.

Obsessive-Compulsive Disorder

OCD is a neurological disorder as well as an anxiety disorder. Thoughts create emotions, and emotions cause actions. This is sequential thinking. When you think a thought, that thought enters the brain and is directed to various lobes. A person who is OCD has a problem filtering thoughts. There is little dismissal of some thoughts because of, we believe, a lack of serotonin in certain lobes of the brain. A person with OCD describes it as "over thinking." Many psychologists describe it as "repetitive thinking" or "intrusive thoughts." Many of our thoughts are minor and can be easily filtered. But a person suffering from OCD is unable to filter even minor thoughts. The thoughts continue to circle, and one cannot get them out of their mind—similar to a recording getting stuck and playing over and over again. The thought may be completely irrational, and the person may know that it is an irrational thought and even wonder why he is thinking it, but he is unable to filter that thought. These intrusive thoughts begin to wear on a person.

In order to deal with these intrusive thoughts, patients often develop rituals. The ritual is developed to dismiss or control unwanted thoughts. Some rituals can be helpful. OCD is not just a mental or emotional problem. It is primarily a neurological problem. Individuals create rituals to satisfy or subdue rapid, reoccurring thoughts. If they do not repeat the ritual, the anxiety becomes overwhelming, resulting in the inability to interact with others effectively.

Areas of Obsession

* Obsession with sex
* Obsession with religion
* Obsession with contamination

These are the three major areas of obsession for OCD patients. Those with OCD may have one or more of these categories and on occasion may have recurring thoughts that are even outside of these categories.

Unwanted sexual thoughts about forbidden, unnatural sexual activities, sexual fantasies about other people, obsessions with whether or not he or she may be gay or homosexual, and obsessions with incest may all fall within the sexual obsessive category. In religion, the most common obsession is to worry if he or she has offended God or committed the unpardonable sin. They may develop intricate superstitions and will tend to be perfectionists trying to live in an imperfect world. Those struggling with contamination concerns will often shower, bathe, or wash their hands several times a day and may refrain from interpersonal activities for fear of being contaminated by another person's germs. A person suffering from OCD sees few gray areas. Most issues are black and white. They may struggle with concepts of right and wrong. Fortunately, OCD can now be controlled reasonably well with medication and therapy.

How Do We Deal With Our Physical, Mental, and Spiritual Illnesses?

How do we cope with what we cannot control? We can do what we can to improve the situation. I am thankful we now have prosthetic limbs for amputees. Whatever we can do medically or psychologically to improve our situation, we should. Luke, in the Bible, was a doctor. I've often wondered if Luke followed Jesus to make sure He was well cared for. The point is, get help and follow the doctor's orders, take medication as directed, and when you feel better, keep taking the medication as directed. It often takes twelve or more weeks for medication to begin to work where a person can feel a difference in mood.

Spiritual Health

When God created man, He created a perfect human being, perfect in every way—perfect body, perfect mind, perfect spirit. But eventually man chose a path other than God's and, as a result, sin came into the world. With sin came consequences. Among those consequences were, most of all, spiritual ones. Sin separates us from God and that separation from God creates many problems, turmoil, and difficulties. The majority of the world is still separated from God and all are still experiencing the problems that come as a result of that separation. We die as a result of separation from God. We experience physical and spiritual death. We get sick, have diseases and abnormalities—all this is the result of man's choosing his way rather than God's way. We have many physical problems. You probably know friends or family who are suffering right now with physical illnesses. We also have mental and emotional illnesses, and we have spiritual sickness as well. All of these are the result of our not initially following the will of God.

Mental and Emotional Illness

The brain malfunctions just as the body and spirit do. These malfunctions create mental problems for us. We have accidents where our bodies are broken or injured, our ligaments are torn, or our bones are fractured, creating pain and difficulty. We have diseases such as cancer; heart blockages; our pancreas doesn't function and we develop diabetes; our lungs do not function correctly and we have trouble breathing. We can suffer from many physical problems.

We have problems with the mind and emotions as well. These problems are so common that we can classify, categorize, and name them. Just as we can have multiple physical problems, we can also have multiple emotional or mental problems. The treatment may be varied. We may be treating more than one mental disorder at a time. The mind may malfunction because of improperly balanced brain chemistry or brain anomalies, which may be the result of birth defects or the brain not developing correctly, or head trauma, which can result from concussion and may cause brain damage. There are diseases or disorders that can cause the brain to be damaged. Our thinking process or thought patterns can become confused, too. We become mentally and/ or emotionally ill as a result.

Stress is also a real problem for our emotional and mental health. Some live under constant stress. This stress over time has an effect on the way we think and our emotional health.

Mind and Emotions

Problems with the mind and emotions may be short-term or long-term. We may be able to heal; then again, we may only be able to cope with the problem. There is an essential mixture of both—trying to do everything we can to lessen the effects of the mental or emotional problems by using psychotropic drugs and/ or through therapy which includes coping skills. Jesus said on one occasion, "Let this cup pass from me" (Matthew 26:3a). Every one of us wishes we could pray and this cup of physical illness or this cup of mental or emotional problems would just vanish. But

Jesus also prayed, "Not my will, but thine, be done" (Luke 22:42, KJV). And it may be that the physical deformity or the mental problem may be what is best for us spiritually. We don't know enough to really know. We know God is in control, so our prayer is always, "God, give me what I need, no matter what it is, here and hereafter. Give me what I need to become the best person, the best servant, the best Christian I can be."

Paul prayed three times to be rid of his thorn in the flesh, but it was not taken away. God did say, however, "I will give you grace to withstand your problem" (2 Corinthians 12:7-9). As Christian therapists we work in two ways. We work to try to eliminate the problem, if possible. We also seek the counsel of man and the grace of God to help cope with our problems. The Serenity Prayer is a beautiful prayer, and one that is on target for our relationship with God and His benevolent grace.

> God, give us grace to accept with serenity
> the things that cannot be changed,
> courage to change the things which should be changed,
> and the wisdom to distinguish one from the other.
>
> ~ Reinhold Neibuhr

There are some things mentally that we will never be able to change, so we learn to cope, just as a person without a limb learns to cope or a person who is blind learns to accept. We learn to accept what we cannot change and live a happy, fulfilled life, despite our infirmities.

As Christians, we have the Great Physician. The Bible teaches that God will give us the grace to bear what we cannot change. Pray fervently. Pray regularly. Pray with great faith and under-standing. Caretakers who seek to help those who have mental and emotional problems must be encouraging. Let us not expect more of those who have mental and emotional problems than they are capable of giving.

Questions

1. What is bipolar disorder?

2. What are symptoms of the manic phase of bipolar?

3. Can bipolar be cured?

4. Discuss the depressive phase of bipolar disorder.

5. Give a definition of obsessive-compulsive disorder.

6. Why do OCD patients develop rituals?

7. What are the most common areas of obsession for OCD patients? Discuss each.

8. How do we learn to cope with what we cannot change?

9. What are the two approaches to eliminating mental and emotional problems?

10. Discuss the "Serenity Prayer" and how it relates to our acceptance of things we cannot change. One real advantage for the Christian is that we have the greatest Physician of all in Jesus, and that we can communicate to Him, and to God through Him, regularly in prayer.

CHAPTER 7

ADDICTIONS:
ALCOHOL AND OTHER
IMPAIRING SUBSTANCES

Biblical Example

Lot was a person who made many bad decisions, and the consequences of those decisions haunted him long after the destruction of Sodom and Gomorrah. The story told in Genesis 19:32-38 features Lot becoming intoxicated and, as a result, on two separate occasions, he has incestuous relations with his daughters. At this time, Lot and his daughters were living in a cave, hiding for fear of being found and put to death. The daughters tricked Lot, getting him drunk and engaging in an incestuous relationship with him.

Belshazzar was at his worst at a drunken feast when the Lord showed him the handwriting on the wall describing the end of his reign (Daniel 5). Samson was called to entertain at a drunken orgy when he literally brought the house down (Judges 16:23-31). The worst things we do in life are often done under the influence of alcohol or other impairing substances. We may not be addicted, but even with the first use of a mind-altering drug, we can make decisions that will haunt us the rest of our lives. Drunkenness is condemned throughout the Scriptures with good reason. It often causes us to do things that we would never do if we were sober.

We have discussed depression, anxiety, and bipolar disorder. In this chapter, we will discuss addictions—specifically, the chemical addictions.

The Bible addresses excessive consumption of alcohol in several passages:

Let us walk properly as in the daytime, not in orgies and drunkenness, not in sexual immorality and sensuality, not in quarreling and jealousy (Romans 13:13, ESV).

Or do you not know that the unrighteous will not inherit the kingdom of God? Do not be deceived: neither the sexually immoral, nor idolaters, nor adulterers, nor men who practice homosexuality, nor thieves, nor the greedy, nor drunkards, nor revilers, nor swindlers will inherit the kingdom of God (1 Corinthians 6:9-10, ESV).

Now the works of the flesh are evident: sexual immorality, impurity, sensuality, idolatry, sorcery, enmity, strife, jealousy, fits of anger, rivalries, dissensions, divisions, envy, drunkenness, orgies, and things like these. I warn you, as I warned you before, that those who do such things will not inherit the kingdom of God (Galatians 5:19-21, ESV).

The problem with substance abuse is that it affects our judgment. It lowers our inhibitions. It's probable that the worst things we do are done under the influence of various substances. For the past thirty years, the majority of my practice has been in helping people with substance abuse problems. I no longer say "alcoholism" because there are so many impairing drugs. I call all these "impairing substances." Alcohol is included, as is any other impairing substance.

Addiction: "A condition [that results] when a person ingests a substance (alcohol, cocaine, nicotine, heroin etc.) or engages in an activity (sex, shopping, gambling, overeating) that can be pleasurable, but the continued use of that act will be compulsive and will interfere with ordinary life and ordinary responsibilities" (Merriam-Webster Dictionary).

This is a broad definition of addiction and why I divided the subject into two sections: substance and non-substance abuse. With substances, there are two problems: the addictive nature of that substance and the psychological addiction. With the other types of addictions, it is primarily a psychological addiction, although there is pleasure associated with any addiction. The main reason people become addicted is because of a pleasurable feeling. An alcoholic drinks for the buzz. It doesn't matter whether you want to get stoned, high, or drunk. Whatever the substance may be, it is giving you some pleasure or you wouldn't use it. Eventually you get to a point where the pain is greater than the pleasure. One begins to make poor decisions. People you love begin to complain. Before long, you will find that your life is full of pain instead of pleasure. The old cliché says that someone who is addicted to a substance will not give up the addiction until the pain is greater than the pleasure is true. One has to "hit bottom" and recognize that on your own, you are powerless over the addiction.

Addictions destroy more lives, families, and friendships than anything else of which I am aware. When one becomes addicted to a substance, that substance becomes more important than anything else.

I have had patients whose first thought in the morning is how they can get their drug today. They'll spend the first part of the day trying to find the money, whether they beg, borrow, or steal it. Then they will spend the latter half of the day trying to obtain the substance and use until it is gone.

One has to be careful when addicted relatives and friends come to your home. The first thing an addict often does is go to your bathroom to check the medicine cabinet. That may be the score for the day. It can happen to anyone. It has happened to me. Some will take anything that alters their reality, no matter what drug it is. If it will give them a high or a low, they will use it.

Alcohol is primarily a depressant drug, and there is a danger there, because many who abuse alcohol are also depressed. Depression may even be why they drink! The result of alcohol use is a depressed feeling. You may be taking a depressive drug to relieve depression. You may become so intoxicated that you don't feel anything, but the overall effect is that of depression.

There are symptoms of substance abuse:

* Being unable to limit the amount of the impairing substance that you use.
* Feeling a strong need or compulsion to use that substance.
* Developing a tolerance to the impairing substance so you need more to feel the same effects.
* Using alone
* Experiencing physical withdrawal symptoms such as nausea, sweating, or shaking.
* Feelings of anxiety when you don't use.
* Not remembering conversations or comments (This is sometimes referred to as "blacking out.") You can have a blackout with many impairing substances. I know someone who will not remember our conversation if he calls after 8:30 p.m. He gets anxious about 7:00 p.m. if he is not near his substance of choice. He even gets irritable and angry. He will find an excuse to leave wherever he is to find his drug of choice; that's how strong an addiction can be. Some people make a ritual of having certain times and places to use a particular drug. As that time of day approaches, you may see a marked difference in their personality if they aren't near their drug.

Those with such addictions exhibit a number of behaviors, including:

* Keeping impairing substances in unlikely places.
* Having legal problems, relationship problems, employment problems, or financial problems, all tracing back to the habitual use of a particular substance.
* Losing interest in family, friends, and other activities that bring most people happiness and pleasure.

All of these are linked to the impairing substance.

Alcohol

We have noted that alcohol is a depressive drug, even though there is a momentary stimulation. It is also one of the most powerful drugs that a person can ever put into his system. We sometimes think that heroin or cocaine is more powerful, but alcohol is among the most powerful and dangerous drugs that anyone can ever use. If someone drinks enough, he will become more and more impaired. When he has imbibed to a certain blood alcohol content (BAC) level, he will go into an alcohol-induced coma. That coma is what some call "passing out," but it is, in fact, a drug-induced coma. The reason one lapses into a coma is because between approximately 0.30-0.40 BAC, one becomes so intoxicated that he is dangerously close to alcohol toxemia, a condition from which thousands of people die each year. The brain shuts the body down by causing a person to go into a drug-induced coma so he cannot drink anymore. Most people who die from alcohol toxemia die because of "chugging." They drink so rapidly that they climb from 0.01 to 0.03 in a matter of minutes. Then they drink more and more until they reach 0.30-0.40 BAC when they pass out, but they have ingested so much that even after passing out the BAC continues to rise. Many of those die from alcohol toxemia. Alcohol is a powerful, controlling, and addictive drug. It is one that enslaves millions of people.

After prohibition, the government decided to try and control, to some extent, the use of alcohol by having "standardized drinks." Keep in mind all alcohol is ethyl alcohol. Beer, wine, liquor—all contain the same alcohol. It is all chemically the same. The way it differs is in the amount of alcohol per drink and what it is made from. One 12-ounce beer contains approximately 5 percent alcohol. It takes a full 12-ounce beer to equal about 9 ounces of malt liquor at 7 percent alcohol, which equals a glass of wine (5-6 ounces), which equals a shot of whiskey (1.5 ounces), which is 40 percent alcohol. So, if you drink a 12-ounce can of beer, or a 7-ounce glass of malt liquor, or a 5-6 ounce glass of wine, or have a shot of whiskey at 1.5 ounces, you are getting approximately the same amount of alcohol. The alcohol is identical. You are going to become intoxicated no matter what you drink, if you drink enough.

Some may say, "I'm not an alcoholic, because all I drink is beer." Most alcoholics do drink beer, and it is highly intoxicating. How many drinks does it take to get a person to 0.08 BAC (the limit for DUI)? There are several factors that determine the amount of alcohol in one's bloodstream at any given time.

(1) Body weight.

(2) The rate at which the alcohol is consumed.

(3) The amount of alcohol consumed.

(4) How recently a person has eaten and the amount eaten.

A chronic alcoholic who has been abusing for fifteen years is likely to have lung and liver impairment. The only way your body eliminates alcohol is via the lungs (approximately 18 percent of alcohol is breathed out) or filtered through the liver (about 80 percent). The remaining 2 percent is eliminated through the pores in your skin. All these factors determine one's blood alcohol content. It takes 2-3 standard drinks to get to 0.08 BAC. It takes one hour for the body to eliminate one drink, provided you are healthy. The process for the liver is called *oxidation*.

Over the years, a chronic drinker may develop cirrhosis as the liver may fail to filter all the impurities of the body. People often succumb to diseases other than alcoholism because they have destroyed one of the body's primary defense and filtering mechanisms—the liver.

With the abuse of alcohol, one's coordination, balance, judgment, and reflexes are impaired. It's no wonder there are approximately 40,000 people killed every year by drunk drivers.

Alcoholics have many domestic problems. People who abuse

often have poor performances at work and school, and they also have an increasing likelihood of committing crimes. Health problems are likely, including liver disease, digestive problems, heart problems, diabetes, sexual dysfunction, menstruation problems, eye problems, birth defects, bone loss, neurological complications, weakened immune systems, and a higher risk of cancer and heart disease. Any of these may be the result of the chronic abuse of alcohol and other drugs.

There are certain noticeable signs and symptoms of a person who is abusing.

(1) Regularly neglecting responsibilities.

(2) Using substances in dangerous situations.

(3) Legal problems.

(4) Continuing abuse, even though it causes distress.

(5) Abusing as a method of relaxing or relieving stress.

(6) Abusing as a sedative to take away the symptoms of depression.

Alcohol is the poorest drug to take for depression. For a few minutes after you drink, you are stimulated. After twenty minutes or so, it shifts to the depressive stage. Warning signs of a person who is chemically addicted include *tolerance* and *withdrawal*. It takes more and more alcohol to get the same effect. This is true of almost every substance people abuse.

Let's look at marijuana for just a moment. Marijuana (THC) is a chemical that is absorbed in fatty tissue. It attaches to the fatty tissues of the brain. A person smokes a joint, the THC is ingested, and it goes through the bloodstream to the brain. Like a magnet, the brain draws in the THC, and it coats the outer surface of the brain. THC, if smoked regularly, builds up because it is not water soluble. It is fat-soluble. That is why it stays in your system much longer. Tests show releases of THC from the brain up to a year after use. That is how long the THC stays in the brain and system. Multiply that by smoking pot multiple times daily, and one begins to develop memory loss that can be permanent.

What About Medical Marijuana?

As with all medicine, we must weigh the benefits with the side effects. Research has found that marijuana helps with glaucoma, nausea, cancer, and other illnesses. This may be like the 1960s, when doctors would administer LSD to psychosis patients because the LSD would cause them to come out of the psychosis mindset and behave normally. But later we found that the patients went into a deeper psychosis after a year or so after being prescribed the LSD. It became an illegal drug. After testing, it showed that the side effects were much worse than the benefits. We should use the most effective drug available, as well as the one with the fewest adverse side effects.

I have come to appreciate people who want to overcome an addiction. It takes courage and strength to get past the denial, which is one reason people continue to abuse. Once the person admits he has a problem, we need to be there to help. We have our own problems and should not be judgmental.

An Un-Sobering Thought

Americans consume 80 percent of all prescription opiate drugs produced throughout the world. That equals 110 tons of prescription opiate drugs consumed in the United States each year. If you add to that all the illegal opiate drugs, the amount would be astonishing.

Questions

1. Is it a sin to become impaired by any substance?
2. What are some of the worst things we do under the influence of various substances?
3. Discuss how drug addiction destroys lives and relationships.

4. Is alcohol a depressive drug?

5. Does it make sense to self-medicate with a depressive drug when you are depressed?

6. What are some symptoms of substance abuse?

7. Is alcohol less addictive than illegal drugs?

8. What is blood alcohol content or BAC? What are the four factors involved in BAC?

9. What are the primary organs of the body that are adversely affected by the abuse of alcohol and some other impairing drugs?

10. What are symptoms you may notice when a person is abusing an impairing substance?

11. How does marijuana affect the brain, and how is it released from the body?

12. Marijuana is legal in many states for medical conditions. Do you believe it is an effective medication for treating certain medical conditions? Why or why not?

CHAPTER 8

NON-CHEMICAL ADDICTIONS

Non-chemical addictions are very common, but they are seldom discussed. They are not necessarily drug addictions, although they do cause the body to produce certain chemicals that can be addictive.

Food Addictions

The idea that a person can be addicted to food has recently gained attention. In the past, we thought that food addictions were primarily psychological, but we are beginning to see that there is more to this type of addiction than simply a craving or urge. Experiments in animals and humans have shown that for some people, the same pleasure center of the brain that is triggered by addictive drugs can also be triggered by certain foods, especially if those foods are high in sugar, salt, or fat content. These foods trigger the release of chemicals that create the same kind of high as drugs. Runners can get this same type of high after running a long distance when they get their "second wind," or "runner's high." This is the body giving you a surge of dopamine, which gives you a euphoric high and enables you to run further than you normally would. The same things happens with food. When you eat, it causes an elevation of dopamine and gives a pleasurable sensation. Like highly addictive drugs, it causes you to want to eat that food more often to repeat the sensation, so you begin to eat not just to sustain life or get nourishment, but to receive the pleasurable sensation again. This is one reason why many people continue to eat after their brain and stomach tells them they are full. They want to repeat the rewarding feeling they get from eating more. It's not usually due to hunger. There are many people whose "hunger switch" does not turn off as quickly as others. There are some who have a very high metabolism and may be able, to some extent, to compensate for these food addictions. The signs of food addiction are many, including developing a tolerance to certain foods and eating more of certain foods high in fat, sugar, or salt. The greater the addiction you develop, the more you build up a tolerance, and as a result you must eat more to get the same high. For some people, their metabolism does increase slightly, which helps to a degree.

People who are addicted to food eat, despite whatever negative consequences they experience. Many times when we eat, we know we are eating at the wrong time, eating the wrong food, eating too much, and eating for the wrong reasons. Proverbs 23:2 (ESV) says, "put a knife to your throat if you are given to appetite." What he is teaching is that the sin of gluttony leads to many kinds of negative consequences. It's much like gambling or addictive shopping—the more you do the more you want to do, until finally you get caught up in the psychological and physical aspects of the addiction. Researchers at Yale developed this questionnaire to discern whether or not one has a food addiction:

(1) Do you end up eating more than you planned to when you started eating a certain food?

(2) Do you select, of all the foods available, a certain food to eat more of because it is more palatable and makes you feel better?

(3) Do you keep on eating certain foods, even though you are no longer hungry?

(4) Do you eat to the point of feeling physically ill?

(5) Do you worry about eating certain types of food, or worry about cutting down on certain kinds of food?

(6) Do you think you're overeating in some areas?

(7) Can you eat certain foods so often or in such high amounts that you leave off those that are the most nutritious?

(8) Do you avoid professional or social situations where you know certain types of food will not be served?

(9) Do you have a problem functioning effectively at school or at work because of eating?

(10) When you eat the same amount of food, does it not produce the same pleasurable experience that it once did?

If you can answer *yes* to these questions, then you may have a food addiction.

Food addictions are not considered as bad as other kinds of addictions—after all, we have to eat! It's absolutely essential. Most of us eat three to six times a day. Some say the more often you eat, and the less you eat per meal, the better you will be.

The chief problem with thinking about gluttony is that we think it is only about food. Certainly that is one of the areas where gluttony is most often demonstrated, but its biblical meaning and definition is broader than that. There are so many people who can't get enough toys. I'm not talking about children; I'm talking about adults. Not only do we want our toys, but we also want the most expensive toys, the best toys, and the most fun toys we can buy. We must be careful that we don't get involved in addictive gluttony in any area of our lives. I remember in college when we began to read *The Screwtape Letters* by C.S. Lewis. In that book he spoke a great deal about the sin of gluttony. It was described as of all the sins throughout history as one of the most disastrous. In Rome, kings enjoyed their food, and it was so readily available, that they would literally gorge themselves, step out of the room, force themselves to throw up, and then go back to gorge themselves again. That is gluttony. There are people today with similar eating disorders. Some are so controlled about their eating, and they will not eat even for nourishment's sake. We call that anorexia. Then there are others who are bulimic. Bulimia is where you eat a normal meal (or gorge yourself), then you excuse yourself to throw up, and then you continue as if you haven't eaten. Many people use this as a method of weight control, but it is a form of gluttony. We can abuse what is good, even if it is necessary for human life. We can abuse and over use it until it becomes a sin. That's true of many pleasures in life. There are things that are legitimate and right, but we abuse and obsess over them, allowing them to become addictive, and they begin to control our lives in a negative way.

In Rome, there was a second part to gluttony, which was extravagance. There are many gluttonous people who have to have everything perfectly to their expectations. They have their favorite foods, and those foods must be prepared in a certain way. We call it gourmet. It must be prepared according to a certain recipe and procedure, and if it isn't it doesn't meet their needs. This kind of gluttony is real. People who demand so much of the finery of life are said to be extravagant and opulent—even ostentatious.

Gluttony is a sin of the flesh. It's a sin of wanting to gratify the body in one way or another. The cure for gluttony lies in a very deliberate effort to restrain yourself from that to which you are addicted. It is a conscious effort, with help, to find the deeper root cause for what you're doing. It does require a moment of conviction to realize what you're doing is hurting you, and that it might be a sin, and to recognize that it is certainly bad for you.

Gambling

Have you ever known anyone who was a compulsive gambler? I have. It's one of the saddest addictions there is. I know people who have literally gone through fortunes gambling. They will bet on anything. They'll bet you $100 that they can quit betting! The more they lose, the more they feel the need to make up for what is lost. "If I'm down $5,000, I need to bet a lot to make it back." The problem is, it's all stacked against you. Even many people who win the lottery wake up two years later and are broke. It is not just a matter of having money, it's a matter of how you use it and how you value it. It matters how you feel about money and what you think about money. The Word teaches us that the love of money is the root of all kinds of evil. People will kill, cheat, steal, and lie for money. It is amazing that we get our priorities so twisted that we feel like we have to chase the unending, never-realized dream. Yet gambling can trick the brain's trigger to give you a good feeling. If you ever win once, that might be the worst thing that could happen to you, because for an obsessive gambler, that specific experience replays over and over in their mind. Psychologically, you want to repeat that good feeling you got from winning.

Another problem is, you cannot adequately talk with a gambler because they're speaking a different language. They are willing to give up something of value for the unlikely possibility that they may gain something of greater value. I have never known a compulsive gambler who didn't end up broke (often more than once). Compulsive gambling is very difficult to treat. It's usually a secret in the hearts and minds and lives of the family or the person who is involved.

One problem associated with gambling is relationship problems. The first relationship problem will be with God. Then it filters to your relationships with your spouse and children. You will have financial trouble, possibly even bankruptcy. Legal problems can occur, including going to jail. Job loss or professional stigmas are also associated with compulsive gambling in the same way they are with drug abuse and alcoholism. Poor general health can result, as well as mental health disorders such as depression and even suicide.

There is a thrill associated with gambling, because you are

taking a bigger and bigger risk. One can become completely preoccupied with gambling. You gamble on football, baseball, or anywhere you can find to place a bet. People have had to move across the country because they owed the wrong people for gambling debts. This lifestyle takes a lot of time from work and family. It takes a lot of concealing and lying. There is a lot of remorse and guilt.

Sexual Addictions

Sexual addictions, previously called hypersexual addictions by the American Psychiatric Association, are limited to people who are 18 and older. It is described as a progressive intimacy disorder. It is compulsive sexual thoughts and actions. Like all addictions, it has a negative impact on those who are involved. The addict usually has to intensify the sexual activity and become more and more bizarre in order to achieve the same thrill. They go from one partner to another, but never find any satisfying relationship because it is not the relationship that matters. It is the power and control of sexual gratification. There are health risks, financial problems, arrests, and other problems with this lifestyle.

The Diagnostic and Statistical Manual for Psychiatric Disorders states "sexual disorders not otherwise specified as distressed about a pattern of repeated sexual relationships involving successive lovers who are experienced by the individual only as a person to be used, never wanting to establish a relationship with that individual." Sexual addicts compulsively search for multiple partners, or a love relationship they never achieve. The compulsive or addictive behavior becomes more intense with time.

It is easier to become sexually addicted today than it was 30 or 40 years ago. The reason is access to internet pornography which, by the way, is the most profitable internet industry today. There are millions of people who spend hours every day looking at sexual websites. It becomes so addictive that they begin watching at work, or miss family functions in order to satisfy their needs.

THE CHRISTIAN AND GOOD MENTAL HEALTH

Sexual addiction is different from other addictions. Eating is necessary to living, and sexual relationships are essential to procreation. Intimacy is a normal action, but God has set the boundaries. Human beings may take what is beautiful and pure, obsess on it, and abuse it until it becomes something that is harmful. Many people choose celibacy, either for cultural, health, or religious reasons, but the vast majority of people do have sexual relationships throughout their lives, hopefully within the confines of marriage as God intends. To abuse and misuse sex takes one of the most sacred pleasures God has given us and makes it harmful. The National Council on Sexual Addictions and Compulsions defines it as "engaging in persistent, escalating patterns of sexual misconduct." People look at others who are addicted to sexual acts and think they are just always looking for a new and exciting relationship, but it's more than that. It becomes an addiction. Whether it is pornography via the internet, a magazine, or pictures, it is acting on the compulsions and going from one partner to the next. It is very devastating. Most people who become addicted lose all of the important relationships in their lives, and they are seldom able to regain them.

Shop Till You Drop

No one knows what causes addictive behavior, but we know that we can become addicted to almost anything. One reason people become addicted is because what they do brings them pleasure. Most will not quit an addiction until the pain becomes greater than the pleasure. Shopping is necessary, as are many other activities, and it can even be enjoyable. My mother used to say she was going "window shopping," and I never knew exactly what that meant. I thought perhaps she was looking for new windows, but she meant that she was going to walk up and down Main Street, looking in store windows at all the things that were displayed.

Recently, research at Rutgers University discovered that ten to fifteen percent of those who become addicted to something actually have a common gene, meaning they may be genetically predisposed. Anyone who becomes addicted to whatever it may be has some gene that can be blamed. Genetics often give us an excuse for our misconduct. I have talked to people who were predisposed to a homosexual lifestyle. There are other people who are pathological or sociological liars. They lie when it would be better for them to tell the truth. They lie about anything and everything. Their first and natural reaction is to lie. My point is, everyone has his or her own predisposition to some sin or another, and we cannot use genetics as an excuse. The only thing that we can live by is the type of conduct that the Bible tells us we are to have—the proper conduct of life. Even though I may be tempted in some direction, I have a choice as to whether or not I will yield to that temptation. That is free will. That is choice. So no matter what the addiction is, you will find people that will tell you that they are predisposed, but that is not an excuse for incorrect behavior.

The technical word for this is "shopaholic" or "reinforced shopping." It does bring pleasure to some people when they shop. But when you start hiding high credit card bills, receipts, and shopping bags, it is a good indication you have an addiction. Shopping addiction may feel positive at first. But those feelings are mixed with anxiety, frustration, and guilt. Sometimes, the anxiety comes from knowing you have spent more than you wanted to or should have, and you are worried that someone will find out what you've spent. So you may act like the alcoholic who walks in yelling and screaming. Why? If you intimidate the other person, they will not say anything about the problem.

The long-term effects of shopping addiction could be overwhelming debt or relationship problems. You might spend more than you can afford to spend. You might shop just because you feel angry or depressed. You may go shopping to feel less guilty about the last shopping spree, but it harms relationships and it is loss of control over behavior.

All addictions have several aspects in common. Many of them are legitimate in and of themselves. When used properly, some are even essential and necessary for life. It is when we begin to abuse them and let them take over our lives and become an addiction that it becomes wrong. In fact, moderation is the word that jumps out from the Scriptures. Most things can be done in moderation, or as they are designed to be done. It is when we abuse and overuse them that they become wrong. Almost all addictions get to the point of being sinful because they do involve harm to us and others. Many people think addictions are an indication of a narcissistic personality, but I do not subscribe to that idea. I do believe that many people who are addicted are selfish as a byproduct of their addiction, and as a result hurt the people around them.

Questions

1. Discuss Proverbs 23:2 and how it relates to food addictions.
2. What is gluttony?
3. Do we consider food addictions as bad as other types of addictions?
4. Is gluttony more than just overeating?
5. Have you ever known anyone who is a compulsive gambler?
6. What is the major attraction of gambling?
7. How are other people affected by compulsive gambling?
8. What is a sexual addiction?
9. Is a sexual addiction about relationship or pleasure?
10. What is the primary motivation for overcoming an addiction?
11. Do all of us have certain predispositions that we must control in order to achieve happiness and be pleasing to God?
12. What are the long-term effects of shopping addiction?
13. Is moderation a desirable quality?

CHAPTER 9

HOW TO OVERCOME
ADVERSITIES AND ADDICTIONS

Biblical Example

The apostle Paul is an example to us in many ways, but I suppose his example is nowhere any stronger than in his willingness to continue despite his handicap. We are not sure just exactly what plagued Paul. It may have been blindness or other sight difficulties. It could have been a speech impediment, possibly even a deep insecurity which made it difficult for him to deal with people personally. Whatever it may have been, he did what each of us must do when faced with an impediment which God allows to continue. Paul prayed three times that his "thorn in the flesh" would be removed, and after receiving an understanding that this impediment was for his own good to keep him humble and Christ-centered, he accepted it as being a useful and necessary imperfection which in some way or another made him a better person.

The first step toward overcoming adversities is to be a true Christian. Try to develop the mind of Christ. Develop the attitude "not my will, but Thine be done." Jesus is our helper and comforter. He said, "I will never leave you nor forsake you" (Hebrews 13:5, ESV). These are among the most comforting words in Scripture. Jesus is always going to be there to see us through any difficulty we may encounter. Hebrews 13:6 (ESV) says, "So we can confidently say, 'The Lord is my helper; I will not fear; what can man do to me?'" Being a Christian changes things for the better on earth and hereafter.

Just prior to His ascension, Jesus said, "I am with you always, even to the end of the age" (Matthew 28:20, ESV). I know God in His wisdom gave us these words to give hope to the hopeless, encouragement to the discouraged, and knowledge that Jesus loves us.

I love the story of Elisha.

Once when the king of Syria was warring against Israel, he took counsel with his servants, saying, "At such and such a place shall be my camp." But the man of God sent word to the king of Israel, "Beware that you do not pass this place, for the Syrians are going down there." And the king of Israel sent to the place about which the man of God told him. Thus he used to warn him, so that he saved himself there more than once or twice.

When the servant of the man of God rose early in the morning and went out, behold, an army with horses and chariots was all around the city. And the servant said, "Alas, my master! What shall we do?" He said, *"Do not be afraid, for those who are with us are more than those who are with them."* Then Elisha prayed and said, "O Lord, please open his eyes that he may see." So the Lord opened the eyes of the young man, and he saw, and behold, the mountain was full of horses and chariots of fire all around Elisha (2 Kings 6:8-10, 15-17, ESV, italics mine).

God's people are victorious because of God's watch, care, and protection. Sometimes, though, we feel like this servant. We feel like we are surrounded by problems and difficulties. They overwhelm us. They cause us fear and anxiety. We wonder why. But by faith, the veil can be lifted and we can see God in all His power—the God who created heaven and earth, and all things in it. We know that those that are with us are more than those that are with them (2 Kings 6:16).

If you look through a concordance, you will find that the statement "do not be afraid" appears 82 times in the Scriptures. "Do not fear" appears 44 times. "I will not be afraid" appears 24 times. "Do not worry"—10 times. If you total those, there are 160 instances in God's Word where He tells us that He will take care of us if we are His. The call is to seek first the kingdom of God and His righteousness, then all the things that we need will be given to us. We need to hear the words of the Lord. "Do not be afraid." "Do not worry." "Do not be anxious." "Do not fear." "If God is for us, who can be against us?"

We must surrender our will to God's will. That is how spiritual renewal begins. That is how we develop the mind of Christ—by loving the Lord with all of our heart, mind, soul, body, and strength. It takes a conscious effort to present ourselves to the Lord, to be used of Him as He wills, and to become a living sacrifice. No matter the condition of our mind and body, we present it all to the Lord to use for His glory and honor.

Learning How to Overcome Adversities

Another part is that we must be grateful—full of joy and gratitude. "Rejoice in the Lord always; again, I will say, rejoice" (Philippians 4:4, ESV). "Do not be grieved, for the joy of the Lord is your strength" (Nehemiah 8:10, ESV). This is another way of saying "Count your blessings, name them one by one. It will amaze you what the Lord has done." By rejoicing in the Lord, He gives us the joy we need to live this life. And He supplies the grace to bear any difficulty we may have. Regardless of our circumstances, our joy and gratitude for what He has done transcends all of our disappointments. As we look back on our lives, we sometimes think it is a steep, uphill battle. But if we look carefully, we can also see how He has been with us every step of the way—He has led us and blessed us in far more ways than we are even aware. When you stop and count your spiritual blessings, it's almost overwhelming. Jesus' forgiveness, the hope we have in Him, the joy and love He provides, and the example He has set—compare these and many other benefits with the empty, meaningless, useless life of the world.

When we are mentally or physically sick or afflicted, we sometimes forget God's past faithfulness. We can only see the difficulties we have or the detours we have taken. But looking back, if we're honest with ourselves, we can see the joy, the purpose, and the victory that God has provided for us. And we realize that though we may have a major illness or affliction, it could always be worse.

> I cried because I had no hat, until I saw a man who had no coat.
>
> I cried because I had no coat, until I saw a man who had no shirt.
>
> I cried because I had no shirt, until I saw a man who had no socks.
>
> I cried because I had no socks, until I saw a man who had no shoes.
>
> I cried because I had no shoes, until I saw a man who had no feet.
>
> I cried because I had no feet, until I saw a man who had no legs.
>
> I cried because I had no legs, until I saw a man who lost his life.
> ~ unknown

The bad things that happen to us in life are in no way to be compared to the wonderful privileges and opportunities and blessings for faithfulness that we will receive hereafter.

We live in a very difficult world. There are those who have lost their jobs and their homes. Some have gone bankrupt, others are getting a divorce. Sickness afflicts many lives. Poverty, loneliness, deformity, addiction, and mental illness—there are many reasons to be depressed, even angry, and to feel alone. But we can be a person, even with our disability, who says to the world, "God is my helper!" The Bible teaches us "The joy of the Lord is your strength" (Nehemiah 8:10, ESV). Proverbs 17:22 (ESV) says, "A joyful heart is good medicine."

A marine by the name of Captain Kirk recently posted on the internet. He said, "we simply need to stop wallowing in our own self-pity, to stop whining and complaining, and realize just how fortunate we really are." He said he watched a man with no feet run in the Olympics. What is our excuse for not living as we should and being an inspiration to the world? We can either be a part of the solution or a part of the problem. We need to cleanse our hearts, and ask the Lord to empower us by His love—to chase out all of our fears, doubts, worries, and anxieties. We need to ask Him to get rid of the anger and the unforgiving spirit so we can become helpers and healers.

Actually, as Christians, we should understand that adversity is going to be a part of our lives. We are the enemies of Satan. When we become Christians, we become targets as Satan tries to discourage and defeat us. Jesus said, "In the world, you will have tribulation. But take heart; I have overcome the world" (John 16:33, ESV). The apostle Paul said, "through many tribulations we must enter the kingdom of God" (Acts 14:22, ESV). The apostle Peter said, "Beloved, do not be surprised at the fiery trial when it comes upon you to test you, as though something strange were happening to you" (1 Peter 4:12, ESV). James, the brother of Jesus, said, "Count it all joy, my brothers, when you meet trials of various kinds" (James 1:2, ESV). After taking spiritual inventory, and believing that we are living as close to the Lord as we can (not that we will ever achieve perfection), then we must realize that every believer, no matter how spiritual or faithful, is going to experience many difficulties, trials, and tribulations. We will expect these adversities, and we will expect that God will help us by His grace to endure whatever comes our way.

Many Sundays we sing songs that were written by a lady who was blinded in an accident as a child. She lived over 90 years, and was very well known in American churches for the beautiful songs that she wrote. Being blind did not deter her from being happy and useful in the kingdom of God. At the age of eight she wrote these words:

> O what a happy child I am, although I cannot see.
> I am resolved that in this world, content I will be.

How many blessings I enjoy, that other people don't.

To weep and sigh because I am blind, I cannot, and I won't.

~ Fanny Crosby

Life sometimes seems unfair. Life's circumstances and people's comments can hurt us and try to take away our joy. But at every crossroad in our life we have choices. We can look behind, or we can look forward in faith, knowing that the providence of God will provide for us.

Never Give Up

When he was seven years old, his family was forced out of their home on a legal technicality. He had to work to help support them. At age nine, his mother died. At 22, he lost his job as a store clerk. He wanted to go to law school, but his education wasn't good enough. At 23 he went into debt to become a partner in a small store. At 26, his business partner died, leaving him a huge debt that took years to repay. At 28, after courting a girl for four years, he asked her to marry him. She said no. At 37, on his third try, he was elected to Congress but two years later failed to be reelected. At 41, his four-year-old son died. At 45, he ran for Senate and lost. At 47, he failed as a vice presidential candidate. At 49, he ran for Senate again and lost. At 51 he was elected President of the United States. His name was Abraham Lincoln.

Life is not always easy or fair. But the most important part is that we never give up. We must keep on doing what is right and living as close to the Lord as we can. He will provide.

God Has a Plan For Your Life: You Have a Special Purpose

"For I know the plans I have for you, declares the Lord, plans for welfare and not for evil, to give you a future and a hope" (Jeremiah 29:11, ESV).

We all go through a process to become the kind of person God can use. We have to be polished. We have to be put into the fire to have the impurities burned away. We have to be able to endure the sadness, sorrow, sickness, and afflictions that come. This process brings about changes in us. It helps us become more understanding, more compassionate, more loving. Yes, God is molding us for the purpose He intends for us. The result will be a man or woman after God's own heart. One who has endured the pressures, difficulties, and pitfalls of life and survived to help others as they make their way through the minefields of their lives. The most important part about living our lives is the way we choose to deal with life's troubles, trials, difficulties, and transitions. Peter committed many sins, but the Lord had a purpose for him. Because his heart was right, and his desire was to do right, he was mightily used by the Lord. On the day of Pentecost, many may have said, "What is this man who cursed and denied doing here?" They might have wondered how God could use someone like Peter in this powerful way. This is the same person who was almost overcome by Satan, and he now stands to face the enemy. They had seen him deny Jesus, curse, become an angry man, and run away. Now this man is ushering in the promises of God for the establishment of His church kingdom. If you had seen Peter during his life, as he was having trouble leaving his worldly habits behind, you might have said, "There's no way he can be used by God."

I have known people in the midst of pain, heartache, sorrow, and loss who have momentarily turned their back on the Lord. Some have denied Him. And, like Peter, some have cursed Him. But once their mind has been restored, as with the prodigal son, they realize the problem is theirs and not God's. They turn their life around. They rededicate and ask for forgiveness. They seek direction and guidance, and they become powerful instruments in God's kingdom. Each of us, in one way or another, goes through this same metamorphosis. From an ugly cocoon a beautiful butterfly is formed. When we shed that cocoon of despair and despondency, bitterness and resentment, we become the beautiful creature God intends us to be, pleasing to Him both inside and out, and we can be used in His kingdom. It all depends on our attitude—what we think about what happens to us and how we rise above our problems and difficulties. Life can get very messy. It can be painful and hurtful, but we should not think God is not on the job. Instead, we need to be glad that we are in the thick of what Jesus experienced—the pain, the suffering, and sorrow, saying always, "Lord, not my will, but Thy will be done." Because as we are placed in the crucible of God's love, and ground with the pestle of His kindness, we get rid of all the negative impurities that plague our life so that we can be the kind of person He wants us to be and to live an inspirational life.

Here I have to repeat 1 Peter 4:12, 13 (ESV):

> Beloved, do not be surprised at the fiery trial when it comes upon you to test you, as though something strange were happening to you. But rejoice insofar as you share Christ's sufferings, that you may also rejoice and be glad when his glory is revealed.

Our lives, and the way we handle our difficulties, is the only sermon many people will ever hear or see. That sermon will have been born out of difficulty, testing, and trials. People watch what you go through. They can be inspired and challenged by how you handle your problems. I believe that the entire fulfillment of our purpose in life hinges on the way we choose to deal with life's difficulties. The difficulties can either make or break us. When we reach a breaking point, we need to hold on and outlast any adversity or difficulty. Keep on going. Cry out to the Lord and He will hear you. We are more than conquerors through Jesus Christ our Lord.

The way we choose to deal with our illnesses and disabilities determines how God can use us to help others as they go through life. In a very purposeful faith and trust in God we believe that He will deliver us and that He will help us. We come to Him in honesty, with all of our failures, our sins, our disappointments, and our hurts. We tell God that we are disappointed—that we wish our lives were different. We ask Him to take us and use us to His glory and honor. Jesus, who went through so many difficult times while on earth, is a High Priest who understands all of our difficulties and problems (Hebrews 4:15). He was wounded for our transgressions. Because of His great sacrifice, living as a mortal man, taking upon himself the burden of all the sins of the world, He understands what we are suffering. He gives us the strength to go on, to do good, and to be His child.

In the fiery furnace of this life, remember that God's will will be done if we allow Him in our lives. He works all things out in our lives for our good, and for His own will. "And we know that for those who love God all things work together for good, for those who are called according to his purpose" (Romans 8:28, ESV). "In him we have obtained an inheritance, having been predestined according to the purpose of him who works all things according to the counsel of his will" (Ephesians 1:11, ESV). After you have done everything you can to correct your problem, difficulty, trial, or tribulation, turn it over to God, and He will grant you the grace and the peace to be victorious.

Pray, Pray, Pray
Prayer changes things, people, and events. Prayer connects us to God, and God to us. Prayer is evidence of faith, and without faith it is impossible to please God (Hebrews 11:6). We have not, because we ask not. Sometimes it's that simple. We just need to ask God to give us the strength to bear our afflictions, understanding to know what we can do, and the courage to do it (James 5:13a). We need to ask for wisdom to know what we can and cannot do (James 1:5). When a trial is beyond our ability, take it to God and go to your knees in prayer. I suppose nothing has driven me to my knees more often than concerns for my family and friends—

seeing those we love taking the wrong direction and making wrong decisions, watching friends and family as they run up one blind alley and down another, searching for happiness, peace, and truth, but looking in all the wrong places. Praying without ceasing means keeping a prayer in your heart all the time—asking for blessings, seeking forgiveness, asking for direction, asking for understanding, praying for God's grace to ever be present, asking Him to rescue us when we fall.

Our Perfect Example

The life of Jesus is the best possible example of prayer. Before every major decision in His life, He prayed. There is no doubt that the Father heard and responded, and gave Him the strength to withstand the humiliation, pain, and sorrow, and even to pass through the valley of the shadow of death. We can have that same confidence, that no matter where we are or what our circumstances may be, we can lift our thoughts to God in prayer, and God will hear and bless. Certainly if Jesus needed to pray as He walked through this life, we need it that much more. In fact, I'm convinced that without much prayer, we cannot successfully live our lives. Are you honest with God? Do you go to Him regularly sharing your fears, doubts, worries, anxieties, frustrations, and pains? That's what He wants us to do. He can handle all of our requests. He can handle the honesty of our hearts. He already knows about the fear, the doubt, the frustration, but our acknowledging it to Him, as we would to an earthly father, is an indication of our faith and confidence in Him and His ability to bring us hope and healing.

If you are suffering with mental or emotional problems or addictions, seek a spiritual counselor to help you. A good Christian counselor can be used by God to help you through your difficult times. If you have physical problems, be willing to follow the directions and instructions of your physician. If you are asked to take medication, take it regularly and as prescribed. Claim your diagnosis; admit your problem. Only then will you be willing to do your part. Do all that you can to help eliminate, accept, or bear your problem. Once we have done all we can, God will do the rest through His grace and mercy. If we are unwilling to do what we know we should (the simple things, like going to the doctor, taking medication, getting rest, etc.), then we cannot expect God and others to do for us what we could be doing for ourselves. Once we are fulfilling our responsibilities, God and others will help supply our needs.

Find a Good Work to Do

God made us to be useful and productive. Until we find something we can do that helps others and is pleasing to God, we will never find our true purpose in life. Each one of us has talents and abilities. Some have one, some have five, others somewhere in between. The job that we find to do may not pay. It might just be a service to others. If we are disabled, we might be able to develop a card ministry, where we send cards to those who are sick and shut in. It might be a phone ministry, where we call those who are hurting. The point is, we need to feel that we are doing something productive to be a blessing to others and a blessing for God.

I have known disabled people who refuse to be victims of their disability. Their lives are a blessing to others because they find their niche. There is nothing that makes us feel more useless than not being involved in the lives of our family and other loved ones in a positive way. I don't know what your talents or abilities are, but I know you have them. I know that when you exercise them, you will find a fulfillment in life that you have not known before. I had a gentleman tell me once, "I am disabled, but not useless." Truer words were never spoken. He was disabled, but he was very useful—a true minister to the needs of others, many of whom were not as disabled as he. Work is not about the job. It's more about the journey. It isn't just about the destination. Work is to help us feel useful and purposeful in life.

Your Gift

God speaks to us through art, literature, poetry, and music. All of these involve talented people—people who are willing to use their gifts to the glory of God and betterment of man. One third of our lives is spent in some kind of work. That work must be spiritual in nature for a Christian. There has to be some meaning or benefit for it to be useful work. I believe that our work can be as meaningful as our worship. Both are essential. I could not work in an occupation that required me to do things that were against God's will.

For most of Jesus' life He worked hard as a carpenter, possibly making chairs, tables, plows, and houses, and by example, showed us the importance of work. Less than three years of His life were spent in public ministry. Most of it was spent in an honorable occupation, doing useful work. When Jesus came to choose His apostles, He chose them while they were at work. It was to the working class that He appealed most.

After man sinned and was driven from the garden, he was told that he must work by the sweat of his brow to earn a living and provide for his family. Honorable work gives us purpose and pleasure. Most farmers will tell you that a farm is not a place just for growing grain, but a place for growing character. Every good occupation helps build our character and our sense of purpose. I don't think perfect character comes to us while we are sleeping, though we spend a third of each day in sleep. Rather, it comes to us as does our physical health—through doing things, exercising, working the mind and the body. Work helps us become the person we need to be. Our Christianity can be demonstrated as much at work as it is in worship. Our true character is revealed, not only in worship, but also in work. Work that is not honest is worse than useless. It destroys the soul.

For most of us, our first job is school. If you are a student, that is your job. Do it well. Take it seriously. Learn as much as you can. Become educated, not only in worldly things, but mostly in spiritual things. Seek to be honest and truthful in all of your endeavors. The Truth is essential. You can be a faithful Christian, and an earnest seeker of truth. In fact, without truth, none of us would ever experience our real purpose. Jesus is the way, the truth, and the life (John 14:6). Good work will bring you a sense of fulfillment and purpose.

Mihaly Csikszentmihlyi, in his excellent book *Flow* (which I highly recommend), asserts that we can never feel completely fulfilled until we find honorable, useful work. He also says that it isn't necessarily the destination of the work, or the achievement of the work that is most important, but simply the experience of the work. The journey may be as important or more important than the destination. Work, if properly understood, can be one of the most meaningful parts of our lives.

A Waste of Time

Although we have seen people generally long to leave their places of work and get home, ready to put their hard-earned free time to good use, all too often they have no idea what to do there. Ironically, jobs are actually easier to enjoy than free time. Because, like Flow activities, they have built-in goals, feedback, rules, and challenges—all of which encourage one to become involved in one's work, to concentrate and to lose one's self in it. Free time, on the other hand, is unstructured, and requires much greater effort to be shaped into something that can be enjoyed. Hobbies that demand skill, habits that set goals and limits, personal interests, and especially inner-discipline to make leisure what it is supposed to be—a chance for re-creation. But on the whole, people miss the opportunity to enjoy leisure even more thoroughly than they do with working time. Many years ago, the great American sociologist Robin Park noted,

"It is in the improvident use of leisure, I suspect, that the greatest waste of American life occurs."

~ Mihaly Csikszentmihlyi

Unfortunately, we spend most of our leisure time wasting it on television that really is not worth watching, or reading books unworthy of our time, or some other entertainment that may make us feel worse, rather than better.

Questions

1. What is the first step in overcoming adversity and addiction?

2. Discuss the story of Elijah and how it relates to relying on the power of God in overcoming adversity. See how often the words "do not be afraid," "do not fear," "I will not be afraid," or "do not worry" appear. What is God saying to us with these admonitions?

3. What does it mean to surrender our will to God's will?

4. How is gratitude important in overcoming adversity?

5. What does the Bible teach about the inevitability of trials and tribulations?

6. Do you believe God has a plan for your life and that you have a special purpose? Look at Jeremiah 29:11.

7. How does God gently lead us through trials and tribulations and develop our character in positive ways?

8. In times of heartache, pain, sorrow, and loss, have you ever momentarily turned away from the Lord? Peter did, but he was able to be used mightily of the Lord later because of his repentance.

9. What place does prayer have in changing things, people, and events, and helping us deal with our adversities.

10. How can staying busy doing good things help us in overcoming adversity and addiction?

11. Do you know disabled people who have refused to be victims of their disability?

12. Discuss how using our time wisely can help in overcoming afflictions.

SOLOMON
HAPPINESS-CONTENTMENT:
LOOKING IN ALL THE WRONG PLACES

Biblical Example

When I think of a biblical example of a happy person, I immediately think of Barnabas, whose name even indicated that he was a person who encouraged other people. What a fantastic talent, to edify, uplift, encourage, and strengthen those with whom we come into contact! Wherever Barnabas went, he tried to encourage people to continue to serve God and to follow the example of Jesus.

Titled "The Encourager," Barnabas even went so far as to be an example of second chances. Sometimes in life we mess up, make mistakes, choose the wrong direction. Few people are willing to forget these missteps in our lives, but some can see beyond to the future potential and are willing to invest themselves in encouraging those who have fallen to get up and begin again. Such was the case with Barnabas and John Mark. Paul did not want to take John Mark on a second missionary journey because of Mark's turning back on the first trip. In fact, a strong difference of opinion developed between Paul and Barnabas. Barnabas took John Mark, and Paul took Silas, and the work and opportunities were doubled as a result of this reasonable resolution to a difference of opinion. Paul eventually changed his mind, and when he was in prison in Rome, close to the end of his life, he encourages Timothy that when he comes to visit him to bring Mark "for he is very useful to me for ministry" (2 Timothy 4:11). Encouragement has many facets and can be expressed in innumerable ways. But truly happy people are always encouragers, uplifting those who stumble and fall, and offering a blessing to those who are weak.

When I think of a truly happy person, I think of one who is kind, considerate, compassionate, and understanding, and one who is able to see the good in others. Certainly in order to be an encourager, one who builds up, one who genuinely compliments, a person has to possess these qualities of kindness and understanding. Often we think of kindness in terms of *deeds* or *actions*, and certainly these are a part of kindness. But kindness is more than just being nice. It is an attitude of mind and heart. It is a characteristic which defines an individual. In Galatians 5:19-21, the apostle Paul gives some traits of human nature, describing them as being "of the flesh." And this seems to be the natural tendency of the world. Works of the flesh come so easily. Hatred, jealousy, selfish ambition, envy—all of these traits are rather self-centered, drawing attention to our own personal needs and rarely ever seeing the needs of others. If we are truly encouragers and truly understand the biblical concept of kindness, which means a pleasant, gentle disposition or a compliant willingness to be of service to others, then we too can be a blessing to others through our encouragement, our recognition of others' abilities and talents, our understanding of their efforts in good causes, and we can compliment them for such behavior. These traits do not come out of a selfish personality, but rather out of a kind, compassionate, loving disposition. Truly the fruit of the Spirit is the spirit each one of us needs to develop: love, joy, peace, patience, kindness, goodness, faithfulness, gentleness, and self control (Galatians 5:22, 23). Fruit of the Spirit is not something we just consciously do, it is what the Spirit of God does in and through us. We need more Barnabases!

We search for purpose and meaning to life. A reason for existence. And sometimes we disappoint ourselves looking in all the wrong places, depending solely on human wisdom. Ecclesiastes describes such a search by a man who seemingly had everything it takes to be happy, every opportunity for happiness, and yet he only found despair and sadness. The book of Ecclesiastes chronicles Solomon's search for happiness and purpose in life. It begins with his detailing the futility of the cycle of one generation after another seeking but failing to find the true meaning and wisdom in life.

In Ecclesiastes 1:12-18, Solomon begins to explore human wisdom. He has already been blessed by God with great reasoning ability and great wisdom. He has used this to search out the values of human wisdom. Wisdom is defined as "a mixture of education and experience." This definition is from a human point of view. Divine wisdom has the added perspective of the blessing of God. We are encouraged to pray for wisdom. Solomon gives his conclusion to human wisdom and describes it as trying to "grasp the wind" (Ecclesiastes 1:17). He says in verse 18, "Such wisdom is the source of much grief and sorrow." Human wisdom can never answer the questions of "Who are we?" "Why are we here?" "Where did we come from?" and "What lies beyond the grave?"

Having rejected human wisdom as the source of happiness and contentment, Solomon continues his quest. In the second chapter of Ecclesiastes we read that he tried to find purpose and happiness through mirth, pleasure, wine, and folly. He also acquired great wealth and achieved great accomplishments. In such pursuits he did not find his answer, but he does give us his conclusion, having searched in all of these wrong places. He says, "Mirth and pleasure are vanity" (Ecclesiastes 2:1). Laughter is madness, mirth accomplishes little, if anything" (Ecclesiastes 2:2). He gives a detailed account of his quest for purpose and meaning. He experimented with wine and folly— what we would define today as the use of drugs and alcohol—and all the supposed pleasurable activities associated with that impaired state of mind.

Using the wisdom he had, seeking to find what was truly

good for people under heaven all the days of their lives, he began to build. He built huge houses for each season of the year. He developed fruitful gardens and vineyards. He had orchards and water pools. First Kings 7:1-12 and 9:15-19 give a detailed ac-count of Solomon's building activities and the acquisitions of his kingdom, including all of his houses and the Temple. He was able to acquire anything he wanted. He could walk down any street and buy anything he saw. Ecclesiastes 2:5-8 details his livestock, silver, gold, treasures, singers, the delights of the sons of men, concubines, sexual gratification, musical instruments, entertainment. He had 700 wives and 300 concubines (1 Kings 11:1-3). He became one of the greatest men in the world from a human point of view, and for a while appeared to be happy (Ecclesiastes 2:9-10). Solomon was greater than anyone who had gone before him and yet with all of his acquisitions and all of his indulgences, he maintained his human wisdom, having all his eyes and heart desired, finding enjoyment in his labor and work. In 1 Kings 10:7, the Queen of Sheba said as she observed his great kingdom, wealth, and extravagant, opulent lifestyle and said, "The half has not yet been told."

But then Solomon's melancholy or depression began to set in. Upon reflection, looking back at all of his accomplishments, he concluded "all was vanity and grasping after the wind. There is no profit under the sun" (Ecclesiastes 2:11). His conclusion was that he had found no pleasure or joy in his labors, no true happiness, no lasting contentment. But his next observation helps us understand why, after his great experiment, he came to this conclusion. Solomon is at a point of hating life. He is depressed and despondent, seeing no purpose or reason for going on. Having everything of this world a person could possibly want, and experiencing all of the pleasures that any person can know, he was empty, depressed, and anxious. After he had reflected upon his earthly wisdom, his madness and folly, he realized his unique opportunity. Who could do more than what he had done? He considered the merits of wisdom, madness, and folly (Ecclesiastes 2:12). He saw that wisdom was better than folly, just as good is better than bad and right is better than wrong. He finally understands the dead-end direction he is traveling. The end result of human wisdom is vanity, "ever learning, never coming to a knowledge of truth." The destination of human pleasure is folly, for both the wise man and the fool eventually die (Ecclesiastes 2:14-16). After death, there is no more remembrance of the wise man than of the fool, and the wise man must leave all that he has acquired to others. Thus Solomon hated life, because all the works done under the sun were very grievous to him. They were vanity and grasping for the wind (Ecclesiastes 2:17). Reflecting upon his great wealth, he came to hate even the labor of his hands (Ecclesiastes 2:18-19) because he has to leave it to someone who comes after him, and because there is nothing more that he can experience or enjoy of a worldly nature. Have you ever tried to buy a present for a person who has everything? Some wealthy individual who doesn't really need anything that you could possibly give him. Solomon had seen it all, done it all, heard it all, and it was, to him, vanity.

He says in Ecclesiastes 2:20-23 that he has to leave his inheritance, all that he has done, to another person, and he doesn't know whether that person will be wise or foolish. How many times do we see children squander the lifetime sacrifice of their parents in a very short time? And, no matter what, someone else will rule over all the results of his labor. He came to despair all his labor. A man with wisdom, knowledge, and skill must leave his heritage to one who has not worked for it, and he doesn't think that's right. This also is evil and great vanity. At the end of his life, what does he have to show for all of his effort? Will he be able to enjoy it beyond the grave? He realizes he can't take it with him, and he says these are sorrowful days and restless nights, grievous works that end in vanity. Looking at life under the sun is another way of saying looking at the sum total of a man's life, trying to find meaning and purpose in all that we do, whether it's our work, our entertainment, our pleasure, whatever. If it is all earth-centered, then at the end of life there is no pleasure in it.

In Ecclesiastes 2:9, however, Solomon gives us the conclusion of a lifetime spent in a search for peace, purpose, happiness, joy, and achievement. His conclusion is: a man should seek to enjoy the fruits of his labor. Work is good, necessary, and essential. There is nothing better than being productive in this life, especially if it is in helping other people, making others' lives better, and serving God. Solomon says on six different occasions that we are to enjoy what we do, using the talents and abilities given to us by God. He does not want us to have a pessimistic view of life, just to "eat, drink, and be merry, for tomorrow we die." He is saying enjoy what you do and what God has given you in terms of talents and abilities. Do what is good and right. That is our best legacy. He realized that the ability to enjoy our labor is a gift from God (Ecclesiastes 2:24). No one can truly enjoy life apart from God. There is no real purpose to life without an understanding of God and without using our resources and abilities to do His will. To those who are good in God's sight—that is, those whose hearts are right—God gives wisdom, knowledge, joy, and understanding. But to the sinner—the person who rejects God as the source of all good things—God gives the work of simply gathering and collecting, hoarding (Ecclesiastes 2:26). For the sinner, his work becomes drab, vanity, grasping for the wind.

Solomon wondered, "Why do bad things happen to good people?" Actually, this is not even a valid question, for there are no "good people." All have sinned and fallen short of the glory of God. "There is none righteous, no not even one." It is true that some people are better than others, and that some people have accepted the grace and mercy and forgiveness of God through

Jesus Christ. But to say that we are good people is a misnomer. It is amazing to me that God blesses any one of us, given our sinful and rebellious lives. But despite all of our sins, failures, and repeated violations of His will, He still loves us and gives us the ultimate blessing of eternal salvation. We should not question the judgment and wisdom of God in His allowing His people to suffer, to be diseased, to have all sorts of problems, and to die. Sometimes the very ailments that we consider to be the worst possible thing for us may in actuality and in eternity be the very best thing for us. These may bring us closer to God and help us to correct areas of our lives that we would never have considered had it not been for what we label as suffering or sorrow. Our prayer should always be, "God, in your wisdom, give me what is best for me. Not my will, but your will be done." Solomon had to learn this lesson.

Sometimes we wonder why evil people become successful by worldly standards. They achieve great wealth, power, and fame, and yet may be extremely evil. The point Solomon is making is that such people have their reward here, and there is no reward at all in the hereafter, but there may well be punishment. Alone and without God we find no eternal meaning to life. This is the first time Solomon has introduced God as being the answer to man's purpose. Until now, he has looked at life strictly without God. He has sought the meaning of life through wisdom, folly, madness, pleasure, wealth, and building. Even when we may be successful in all of these areas, the reality of life and death can cause us to be depressed, empty, anxious, and without eternal purpose. So he concludes that life without God is all vanity and grasping for wind.

But with God, who gives wisdom and knowledge and joy to us, we can enjoy everything that is good in life. The good work that we do, the talents that we use, the sacrifices we make become pleasurable—in fact, as pleasurable as the wealth we gain. There is now purpose and meaning for life. Ecclesiastes 2:26, "God gives wisdom and knowledge and joy to a man who is good in his sight." Being and doing good in God's sight thus becomes our purpose and the source of true meaning, happiness, and contentment. Alone and without God we find no eternal meaning to life. Life becomes vain and pointless. That's why 41,000 people took their lives in our country last year, and why we spend over $300 million on fortune tellers. It's the reason why so many people struggle just to maintain their sanity.

Yes, we live in an age of anxiety and depression, and a constant struggle to find meaning and purpose. We have tried all the false paths the world has to offer and still, we are empty. Still we cry, as did Solomon, "Vanity, vanity, all is vanity!" Look at America today. The best fed, best educated, best housed, and most prosperous and affluent people ever to live on the earth. Yet, still most have not found peace and purpose. We have the best army, one of the best governments, the highest standard of living, but we are still empty and our world is still beset with the same problems as always: war, crime, hatred, greed, malice, poverty. We complain about many lost, wandering people. The truth is, they are products of an earth-bound mentality, of a worldly wisdom search for truth, purpose, and meaning. Jesus said, "Man shall not live by bread alone" (Matthew 4:4). It takes more than even the necessities of life such as food, shelter, or clothing, to find peace and purpose. Science, materialism, art, music, companionship all have a natural place in our lives, but they are not ends in themselves. After all, when we have all of these, many are still empty and alone. Our world has changed little since Solomon penned the words in Ecclesiastes. Ours is still a world of sin, sorrow, and death, and a world very much in need of God and an understanding of His Son Jesus Christ. Solomon said in Ecclesiastes 12:13, "The conclusion of the matter is this: Fear, respect God, and keep His commandments, for this is the whole of man."

"No one knows what tomorrow may bring. The nice place to be is in someone's thoughts. The safest place to be is in someone's prayers. And the very best place to be is in the hands of God."

~ unknown

Questions

1. What is our primary reason for existence?

2. What are two kinds of wisdom?

3. Is worldly wisdom a good standard to build a life on?

4. With all of the power and possessions that Solomon had, why do you think he was depressed and melancholy?

5. In Ecclesiastes 2:20-23, what is the major reason for Solomon's depression?

6. Why do bad things happen to good people?

7. Have we as God's people learned the true meaning of "Not my will, but Thy will be done"?

8. Does the world's path to meaning and purpose bring us anxiety and depression, or peace and comfort?

9. How can we overcome our earthbound mentality and desire for worldly wisdom (Matthew 4:4)?

10. Discuss Solomon's conclusion (Ecclesiastes 12:13).

CHAPTER 11

HAPPINESS IS

It is difficult to define happiness. There are variables. As the search for happiness becomes deeper, more scientific, and even more emotionally centered, certain aspects become apparent. Sonja Lyubomirsky describes happiness as "the experience of joy, contentment, or positive well-being, combined with a sense that one's life is good, meaningful, and worthwhile." Sonja Lyubomirsky is a leader in the field of positive psychology. Martin Seligman, one of the leading researchers in positive psychology and author of the book *Authentic Happiness*, describes happiness in three parts: pleasure, engagement, and meaning. Pleasure is the "feel-good" part of happiness. Engagement refers to living a good life (work, family, friends, hobbies). Meaning refers to our strength—to contribute to a larger purpose. He says that all three areas are important, but of the three, engagement and meaning make the most difference in living a happy life.

The Greek word for happiness is *eudemonia*, which means "living well and doing well." Happiness, from an ethics point of view, is a self-realization theory that makes happiness, or personal well-being, the chief good for man. There is a difference between the Bible's view of happiness and our culture's view, though we do find similarities. Author and minister Greg Laurie draws key distinctions between the Bible's view and culture's view of happiness. He says that true happiness is independent of our circumstances. It is self-contained, regardless of what is happening internally or externally. He believes it is possible to be a truly happy person and genuinely blessed by God. But as we can see by looking at our world, this idea stands in sharp contrast to the view of the majority of the world. The world's happiness depends on good things happening regularly in our life. If we have a good job, a nice home, a nice car, good health, and other external things, then we can be happy. Some people define happiness as the equivalent of wealth. Certainly there are wealthy people who are happy, because they have learned how to use their wealth in constructive ways. But we must be very careful about what we ask for. The love of money is the root of all kinds of evil and does not necessarily produce happiness.

A survey by Gallup, a national opinion research center, has found that truly spiritually committed people are twice as likely to report being happy than less religious people. Religious people tend to be happier people, but not all religious people are godly people. Happiness comes from discovering God's plan for our lives. This is our real purpose for being here on earth. This comes not from just knowing ourselves, but from knowing God. "Happy are the people whose God is the Lord" (Psalm 144:15, NKJV).

Father Knows Best

God created us and, as a result, knows what is best for us. He understands us better than we understand ourselves. His Word is our compass, our guide, and a light for our path. C.S. Lewis stated it this way in *Mere Christianity*, "God designed the human machine to run on Himself. He is the fuel our spirits were designed to burn, or the food our spirits were designed to feed on—there is no other." God has the keys to happiness, and they are revealed in His Word, the Bible. If you want to know how to be happy, go to the Sermon on the Mount—to the beautiful attitudes Jesus has described there. As these attitudes are developed in our hearts, they produce happiness and peace. These attitudes are opposite to the world's view of happiness, which believes that getting, owning, and possessing are the keys to happiness.

- Blessed are the *poor in spirit*, for theirs is the kingdom of heaven.
- Blessed are those who *mourn*, for they shall be comforted.
- Blessed are the *meek*, for they shall inherit the earth.
- Blessed are those who *hunger and thirst for righteousness*, for they shall be satisfied.
- Blessed are the *merciful*, for they shall receive mercy.
- Blessed are the *pure in heart*, for they shall see God.
- Blessed are the *peacemakers*, for they shall be called sons of God.
- Blessed are those who are *persecuted for righteousness' sake*, for theirs is the kingdom of heaven.
- Blessed are you when *others revile you and persecute you* and utter all kinds of evil against you falsely on my account. Rejoice and be glad, for your reward is great in heaven, for so they persecuted the prophets who were before you

  (Matthew 5:2-12, ESV).

We certainly do not want to overstate the issue. There are events that are beyond our control that come into the lives of every Christian and bring us temporary sadness and heartache, but because we are Christians and have the power of God working in us, these conditions are only temporary. Soon we are back to feeling the good and positive aspects of life.

There are simply some things that wealth, money, and power cannot buy. And there are other things it can buy. Money can buy you a bed, but it can't buy you a good night's sleep. It can buy you a book, but it can't buy you a brain. It can buy you a house, but it can't buy you a home. It can buy you medicine, but it cannot buy you health. Money can buy you amusement, or entertainment, but it cannot buy you happiness.

Henry Ward Beecher said, "the strength and happiness of man consists in finding out the way God is going, and going in that way, too." God wants us to be happy. The Bible teaches "may all who seek you rejoice and be glad...let the hearts of those who seek the Lord rejoice...rejoice in the Lord, O you righteous, and give thanks...make a joyful noise to the Lord, all the Earth; break forth into joyous song and sing praises...be glad and rejoice with me... rejoice in the Lord always; and again I will say, rejoice...rejoice always, pray without ceasing, give thanks in all circumstances" (Psalm 40:16; 70:4; 105:3; 97:12; 98:4; Philippians 2:18; 4:4; 1 Thessalonians 5:16-18, ESV).

Why?

Why are so many people unhappy? It is because they leave God, and His definition of happiness, out of the equation. Abraham Lincoln said, "people are about as happy as they make up their minds to be." The Roman emperor Marcus Antonius said, "No man is happy who does not think himself so." Happiness cannot be found in having everything we want, because we often want what is bad for us. Henry Van Dyke said, "It is better to desire the things we have, than to have the things we desire." Solomon said the same thing:

> "And whatever my eyes desired I did not keep from them. I kept my heart from no pleasure, for my heart found pleasure in all my toil, and this was my reward for all my toil. Then I considered all that my hands had done and the toil I had expended in doing it, and behold, all was vanity and a striving after wind, and there was nothing to be gained under the sun." (Ecclesiastes 2:10, 11, ESV).

Some of the most miserable people I know are wealthy. Some of the happiest people I know are poor. Charles Spurgeon said, "Happiness is being satisfied with what we have got, and with what we haven't got." It was Paul, the great apostle, who said,

> "But godliness with contentment is great gain, for we brought nothing into the world, and we cannot take anything out of the world. But if we have food and clothing, with these we will be content. But those who desire to be rich fall into temptation,

into a snare, into many senseless and harmful desires that plunge people into ruin and destruction. For the love of money is a root of all kinds of evils. It is through this craving that some have wandered away from the faith and pierced themselves with many pangs" (1 Timothy 6:6-10, ESV).

So long as our search for happiness is confined to material things, or certain people, or idealistic circumstances, we will never be happy. People often say, "If only I had more money I would be happy." Or a bigger house, or a nicer car, or a beautiful wife or handsome husband, or if I could change the way I look, I would be happy. None of these things bring happiness by themselves. Often they bring sadness and sorrow. I have seen people live their lives running from one place to another, thinking there is a destination that will make them happy. "If only I could live in _____, I would be happy." Happiness is not a destination. A person must learn to be happy wherever they are. Jesus said, "I came that they may have life and have it abundantly" (John 10:10, ESV). "These things I have spoken to you, that my joy may be in you" (John 15:11, ESV). It is wonderful that we can have the joy of Jesus in us.

What is happiness? At least a part of it is meaning, purpose, contentment, inner peace, well-being, hope, belonging, love, caring, giving...but we will never find it by looking in all the wrong places. We won't find it by thinking that our next purchase, our next entertainment event, our next relationship, our next vacation, or our next job will make us happy. Happiness is not just external. It is not completely dependent on circumstances or situations. Happiness comes from within—from fulfilling our real purpose in life. Think for a moment about what makes you happy. What makes you smile and brings joy to your heart? Chances are, it's the small blessings of life combined together to make you truly rich in the things that count.

Deitre Uchtdorf, German aviator and religious leader, says, "So often we get caught up in the illusion that there is something just beyond our reach that would bring us happiness—a better family situation. But the true miracle of faith in God is not that He changes the circumstances of your life, but that He changes you and your heart to meet those circumstances." We can learn to handle the adverse blows of life without blame or bitterness.

Harvard University conducted a survey of 173 graduates in the early 1940s. The study continued for years and was reported in the American Journal of Psychiatry. It said that one predictor of *well being* through life is the ability to handle emotional crisis maturely.

Happiness Is More About Others Than Ourselves

True happiness comes by thinking less about ourselves and more about others. Genard Rinland, director of child behavior research, found that the happiest people are those who help others. In this study, they label people in two ways: happy and unhappy. Then, they labeled the same people selfish or unselfish, and categorized the results. The study found that people labeled happy were also labeled unselfish. He wrote that those whose activities are devoted to bringing themselves happiness are far less likely to be happy than those whose efforts are devoted to making others happy. The Bible says something like that: "Do unto others as you would have them do unto you." We call it the Golden Rule. No, getting what we want does not always make us happy. In fact, it can often have the opposite effect. Six weeks before Elvis Presley died, a reporter asked him, "When you first started playing music you said that you wanted to be rich, famous, and happy. Are you happy?" His reply was, "No, I'm lonely as hell."

Author, columnist, and teacher Adair Lara offers this good advice:

"Happiness is listening to the shout of children playing basketball in the fading light, and feeling your spiritual eyes just from having paid attention. Happiness is an attitude, not a condition. It's cleaning the Venetian blinds while listening to an aria. Spending a pleasant hour organizing your closet. Happiness is your family assembled for dinner. It's the present—not the distant promises of a 'someday when.' How much luckier we are, and how much more happiness we experience if we can fall in love with the life we're living. Happiness is mostly a choice. Reach out, for it is at the moment it appears, like a balloon drifting seaward in a bright blue sky."

The source is unknown for the following list of activities that can bring happiness:

(1) Give something away (no strings attached).

(2) Do a kindness (and forget it).

(3) Spend a few minutes with the aged (their experience is a priceless guidance).

(4) Look intensely into the face of a baby (and marvel).

(5) Laugh often (it's life's lubricant).

(6) Give thanks 1,000 times a day (isn't enough).

(7) Pray with faith.

(8) Work with vigor.

(9) Plan as though you'll live forever (because you will).

(10) Live as though you'll die tomorrow (because you will on some tomorrow).

Some Essential Factors in Happiness

In order to be happy, we must have good values—wisdom, knowledge, courage, humanity, love for God, love for others, love for ourselves. We must be kind, generous, curious, and compassionate. Without true virtue, we will never be happy. These virtues are all described in the Bible. Fairness, moderation, forgiveness, self-reliance (to an extent), appreciation of beauty and excellence, understanding of God and all that He has created, kindness, faith, hope, and love. Humor, a genuine smile, hearty laughter, resilience—all of these are elements of happiness.

Resilience

One of the most important elements of happiness is resilience. Ask the question, "What has my pain taught me about life?" Has it helped you appreciate the good things that come your way? One of the most resilient people I know died at the age of 98. All of her children passed before she did. She lived a very simple life in what could be described as a shack. Up until the last few years of her life, she cooked on wood-burning stoves. She had no running water. She had no indoor toilet facilities. But she was one of the happiest people I have known. As I often talked to her, she would describe the many problems she had experienced in her life—the deaths of her first and second husbands, the deaths of her children, the sicknesses she had encountered, and the sadness of being taken advantage of. But she always bounced back. Whenever I saw her, she had a smile, a kind word, and optimistic thoughts. Resilience is important in our quest for happiness. True, meaningful resilience comes from a faith in God and an understanding that we all go through pain and suffering. But God provides the tools to cope with the problems of life. We can't get stuck in yesterday or tomorrow, but we must live today, for the problems of today are enough.

> "Therefore do not be anxious about tomorrow, for tomorrow will be anxious for itself. Sufficient for the day is its own troubles" (Matthew 6:34, ESV).

The Science of Happiness

The way we think affects our body and our health. Depression and anxiety are the opposite of happiness. When we are under constant stress, our cortisol levels are affected. Cortisol has to do with the kidneys and is associated with stress responses. Prolonged stress impairs our cognitive functions. It suppresses our immune system. It increases our risk of deeper depression or anxiety. Anxiety and depression create sleep challenges. When our sleep is interrupted, it affects our health. Lack of sleep is one of the contributors to obesity. Lack of sleep produces fatigue and acerbates many health problems. Guilt, remorse, depression, and anxiety all affect our sleep patterns.

The Bright Side of Life

Those who are happiest have learned the secret of optimism—expecting the best, not the worst. Dr. Martin Seligman in his book *Learned Optimism* states that those who develop optimism live longer and are healthier, and have healthier relationships. Optimism is the opposite of pessimism, which is a distraction to happiness. Every time a negative thought enters our mind, we should try to consciously replace it with a positive one. The mindset of pessimism is one of the major barriers to happiness. I like Dr. Phil's response to those who have pessimistic, negative thinking. He usually says, "How's that working for you?" The answer to that rhetorical question is always, "Not very well." I have counseled with many people over the years whose primary barrier to happiness is negative thinking. Every thought immediately goes to its worst possible outcome. They believe that something they have done causes hurt and harm to others, when they haven't been involved in the situation at all. But they are constantly apologizing, when they have done nothing that would affect what they are worried about. But their negative thinking and pessimistic view inflates their sense of power over others and over events. God wants us to have a realistic view of ourselves. He also wants us to be filled with joy and happiness. He expects us to be a blessing to others, not a burden. A pessimistic, negative person will never achieve complete happiness.

Empathy

Empathy begins with an awareness of another's feelings and emotions—being able to relate to the conditions of their life. Empathetic people are likely to notice someone else's feelings and to be sympathetic towards them. Empathy is a key element in compassion. Empathy precedes compassion. When we feel empathy for someone, we are receiving and processing emotional information about them and their situation. This allows us to know them better and to be better able to help them. Helping others is what Christians are all about. It's one of the elements of happiness. Those who are unable to get in touch with their own feelings are not likely to have a sense of conscience or empathy. They may feel no remorse or guilt for causing harm to others. Studies show that people who lack empathy and conscience are narcissistic and are often unlikely to respond to treatment.

Gratitude

One of the most important elements of happiness is gratitude. Gratitude promotes the enjoyment of positive life experiences. Expressing gratitude enhances self-worth and self-esteem. When you realize how much people have done for you, and how much you have accomplished because of them, you feel more confident. Gratitude helps people cope with stress and trauma. When we express gratitude, it encourages good behavior. Grateful people are more likely to help others. As we become aware of the kind and caring acts of others, and feel compelled to reciprocate, we experience more happiness.

People who are grateful are less likely to be materialistic. You'll appreciate what you have and become less centered on acquiring more things. Expressing gratitude also helps avoid the tendency to compare ourselves with others. If we are genuinely grateful for what we have (family, health, food, shelter, clothing, etc.), then we are less likely to envy what others may have. Sonja Lyubomirsky, in writing about positive psychology, states that the practice of gratitude is incompatible with negative emotions, and may actually deter such feelings as bitterness, anger, and greed. She further says that gratitude helps us with hedonic adaptation. Hedonic adaptation is illustrated by our remarkable capacity to adjust rapidly to any new circumstance or event in our lives. Gratitude is essential in achieving happiness and in being a true Christian.

Forgiveness

Another key element of happiness is forgiveness. There can be no true happiness in a person's life as long as they hold on to past hurts and mistreatments, whether real or perceived. We must develop an attitude of letting go of the past. We must forgive for good, never looking back on the mistreatment. Forgiveness must be on a mental and spiritual level. It must be relational, in that we must forgive everyone who may have offended or hurt us.

If God in His grace and mercy can forgive us for all of the sins and mistakes of our lives, then surely we should be able to forgive others who often sin and use bad judgment, just as we do. Forgiveness is not saying that what was done to you is okay. It may have been a sinful act on the part of another. But you are going to do what you can do to feel better, because forgiveness is as much for you as it is for the offender. One definition says it well: "Forgiveness can be defined as peace and understanding that comes from blaming that which has hurt you less, and taking the life experience less personally, and changing your grievance story to learn what you can from it." Forgiveness helps heal hurt feelings. Lessen your expectation of things and emotions from other people that they do not choose to give you, or may be unable to give you. Remember that a life well lived is your best understanding of "heaping coals of fire on their head" (Proverbs 25:22; Romans 12:20). Instead of focusing on your wounded feelings, and giving the person who has harmed you power over you, learn to love and forgive them. Forgiveness is about your personal power.

Concluding the Matter

I believe that Christians should be happy. John 10:10 (ESV) reads, "I came that they may have life and have it abundantly." Why shouldn't we, as Christians, be happier? God has forgiven our sins. He has promised us peace, joy, and purpose. Christians should shine like a bright star in a dark world. We are called to be the light of the world—an example to others. What produces happiness, fulfillment, success, peace, and joy? I believe it is getting along well with God and others. It's living rightly.

The only way we can know how to live is to understand the Word of God and to appropriate its principles to our lives. Happiness comes from loving God, loving others, and loving ourselves—certainly from applying the Golden Rule. We are to love God with all our heart, mind, soul and strength, and to love our neighbor as ourselves. Bitterness, hatred, and resentment destroy happiness. People who like to fuss and fight are rarely happy. Happiness comes from not only loving others, but also being empathetic, compassionate, and forgiving. This is the opposite of narcissism and self-centeredness. Jesus said that He "came not to be served but to serve" (Matthew 20:28, ESV).

Live Today

Some are unhappy because they live in the past; others are unhappy because they live in the future. Paul encourages us to live in the moment. "...forgetting what lies behind and straining forward to what lies ahead, I press on toward the goal for the prize of the upward call of God in Christ Jesus" (Philippians 3:13, 14, ESV). He also said, "I know whom I have believed, and I am convinced that he is able to guard until that Day what has been entrusted to me" (2 Timothy 1:12, ESV). Such confidence in our future produces happiness. Let's live one day at a time. Not yesterday, not tomorrow. Just today. Sufficient to every day are the problems for that day (Matthew 6:34).

Our decisions definitely affect our happiness. Every decision we make will either add to or subtract from our happiness, peace, and purpose. We can only be truly happy and know our real purpose for existence if we are true Christians. By coming to the Lord through faith, confession, repentance, and baptism, we are added to His church and become one of His children, receiving the Spirit as a guide, developing the fruit of the Spirit in our lives. "But the fruit of the Spirit is love, joy, peace, patience, kindness, goodness, faithfulness, gentleness, self-control; against such things there is no law" (Galatians 5:22, 23, ESV). Paul is reminding us that a person who possesses the spirit of God and is directed through God's Word will have these qualities as a part of his or her life. A simple rule for Christians helps with happiness: avoid *addictions*, *obsessions*, and *compulsions*. Practice *moderation* in all good things. We only have one life; let's learn to live it being happy.

Questions

1. What is the definition of happiness from the Greek?
2. Is there a difference between the Bible's view of happiness and our current culture's view?
3. Are truly spiritual people more likely to be happy? Why?
4. Can happiness be bought? Why or why not?
5. Can people who are poor, sick, and rejected be happy?
6. Can people who are rich, educated, and influential be sad and depressed?
7. Why do you believe so many people are unhappy today?
8. Do we have to have everything we want in order to be happy? Why or why not?
9. Is our ultimate happiness solely dependent on people, places, and things?

10. What are some things that make you the happiest?

11. Why is gratitude essential to happiness?

12. Why is forgiveness a key element of happiness?

13. Do you believe that Christians should be happy and content? Why?

14. Can living in the past or the future bring us true happiness?

CHAPTER 12

SUICIDE

Suicide is a very difficult study. It is difficult for many reasons. Normally, when we discuss suicide, we are emotional because someone we love and care about has decided to take their own life. It is difficult because there is not much said in the Bible about suicide, but there is enough, I think, that we can come to some conclusions. It is very important that we realize there are many people who attempt to take their lives every year. In fact, over 500,000 people a year in the United States attempt suicide. Of that half million, 36,000-plus end up succeeding in taking their own life. There is something going on in the mind, heart, and life, causing incredible pain, resulting in someone taking their own life every 17 seconds. There are four times as many men who succeed in completing suicide as women, and the question most often asked is, "Why would a person take their life?" This question haunts us. How does someone get to the point where they would want to end their own life?

There are six reasons listed for suicide in the *Diagnostic and Statistical Manual for Mental Health Professionals*. I suppose one could break these down even further, but these six are the major reasons listed:

(1) **Major depression**. Ninety percent of all people who commit suicide have a diagnosable mental or emotional illness, and most are severely depressed. Some also have acute anxiety.

(2) **Psychosis**. Psychosis means a person may be hearing and

seeing things that do not exist. Their thinking has led them to a place where they are not in touch with reality. When a person seeks counseling, one of the first things the counselor does is test their cognitive awareness. We want to know if they know where they are, why they are there, if they know what day and time it is. Their awareness of reality is essential to helping those with mental or emotional problems.

(3) **Impulsiveness.** There are some people who are extremely impulsive. Those we define as impulsive are among those who are often addicted to drugs. They are risk-takers. This results in more wrong decisions and decisions that can be fatal, decisions that can cause enormous regrets. Of the 36,000-plus people who take their own lives every year, there are probably half again as many who could be classified as having committed suicide if we knew all of the true circumstances. Car wrecks, other types of accidents such as hunting and fishing accidents, that are often disguised as accidents but because of the history of the individual could possibly be classified as suicides.

(4) **People are crying out for help.** They don't know what is wrong with them; they just know something isn't right. Some may even get to the point where they have irrational opinions as to what their problem could be. Others develop a sense of hopelessness and feel there is no answer to their problem except to leave this world. For these, suicide is a cry for help. There are many who attempt suicide who do not want to die, but want to make everyone aware of how much pain they are experiencing, but unfortunately go too far and take their own life when actually they were just crying out for help.

(5) **There are those who psychologically want to die.** This is the ten percent that, if you analyzed them, you could

probably say they are not mentally or emotionally ill. They would pass all the tests. They are rational, calm, and they know what they are doing. They have just decided, for whatever reason, they don't want to live any longer. There is a sense of fatalism in their personality.

(6) **There are some who make mistakes in life they do not want anyone else to know about.** When people find out about their mistakes, they panic and sometimes take their own life. This is sad because if everyone knew everything about any one of us, we would probably feel some shame and guilt. There are no perfect people. We all sin and fall short of the glory of God. Each person makes many mistakes in their life. We all do and say things that we wouldn't want anyone else to know, but sometimes everyone else does find out, and we must learn to deal with that reality.

There are others who cannot accept loss, especially major loss—the loss of someone very close or dear to them, or perhaps the loss of their financial wealth. During the Great Depression there were many people who completed suicide because overnight they had lost all of their material possessions. The reasons a person may have for completing suicide can either be real or perceived reasons. They can actually be factual problems or simply problems in the mind of the person who sees no other way out than suicide.

Biblical Examples of Suicide

First Samuel 31:3-6, ESV, says "The battle pressed hard against Saul, and the archers found him, and he was badly wounded by the archers. Then Saul said to his armor-bearer, 'Draw your sword, and thrust me through with it, lest these uncircumcised come and thrust me through, and mistreat me.' But his armor-bearer would not, for he feared greatly. Therefore Saul took his own sword and fell upon it. And when his armor-bearer saw that Saul was dead, he also fell upon his sword and died with him. Thus Saul died, and his three sons, and his armor-bearer, and all his men, on the same day together." This account reveals several reasons as to motives in Saul's mind. He had disobeyed God on several occasions and as a result God had withdrawn His care for him. Also, at this point Saul was defeated by his enemies. He knew if he were captured he would be tortured in unspeakable ways. His would be a very slow and painful death.

In Matthew 27:3-5, ESV, we read of the suicide of Judas. "Then when Judas, his betrayer, saw that Jesus was condemned, he changed his mind and brought back the thirty pieces of silver to the chief priests and the elders, saying, 'I have sinned by betraying innocent blood.' They said, 'What is that to us? See to it yourself.' And throwing down the pieces of silver into the temple, he departed, and he went and hanged himself." This second account of suicide is the first one in the New Testament. Judas had committed an act for which he could not in his own mind find forgiveness. The Bible does say he was sorry for what he had done, that he did repent. He went back and even tried to make reparation and restitution, but the priests would not accept it. When he realized the horrible thing he had done, he took his own life.

Just one chapter before, in Matthew 26:24, this statement is made about Judas: "...but woe to that man by whom the Son of Man is betrayed! It would have been better for that man if he had not been born." In what way would it have been better? Well, probably in more ways than we are aware of. But it would have been better that Judas had not been born because Judas had made a conscious decision to betray the Lord and, as a result of that decision, and the incredible pain he felt, he took his own life.

Judges 9:50-54 tells us of Abimelech, a ruler of Israel. "Then Abimelech went to Thebez and encamped against Thebez and captured it. But there was a strong tower within the city, and all the men and women and all the leaders of the city fled to it and shut themselves in, and they went up to the roof of the tower. And Abimelech came to the tower and fought against it and drew near to the door of the tower to burn it with fire. And a certain woman threw an upper millstone on Abimelech's head and crushed his skull. Then he called quickly to the young man his armor-bearer and said to him, 'Draw your sword and kill me, lest they say of me, "A woman killed him."' And his young man thrust him through, and he died." Here is a person who did not strike the fatal blow, but he commanded someone else to kill him. It is listed as a suicide because it was his desire and command and he, being in authority, ordered another person to carry it out. I will leave it to others to make the final decision as to whether or not this was a suicide or murder, or both.

A few chapters later we read about Samson's suicide during a Philistine banquet. "And when their hearts were merry, they said, 'Call Samson, that he may entertain us.' So they called Samson out of the prison, and he entertained them. They made him stand between the pillars. And Samson said to the young man who held him by the hand, 'Let me feel the pillars on which the house rests, that I may lean against them.' [Remember, he was blind at this time.] Now the house was full of men and women. All the lords of the Philistines were there, and on the roof there were about 3,000 men and women, who looked on while Samson entertained. Then Samson called to the Lord and said, 'O Lord God, please remember me and please strengthen me only this once, O God, that I may be avenged on the Philistines for my two eyes.' And Samson grasped the two middle pillars on which the house rested, and he leaned his weight against them, his right hand on the one and his left hand on the other. And Samson said, 'Let me die with the Philistines.' Then he bowed with all his strength, and the house fell upon the lords and upon all the people who were in it. So the dead whom he killed at his death were more than those whom he had killed during his life" (Judges 16:25-30, ESV). Samson, facing great betrayal of God, realizing God had given him so much and he had wasted his talent and time—this had to have been a part of his decision to take his own life. The Philistines had tricked him and blinded him, and he was seeking retribution for their actions. Samson, who took his own life, is also listed in the "hall of faith" in Hebrews 11:32.

First Kings 16:15-18 tells the story of the death of Zimri. "In the twenty-seventh year of Asa king of Judah, Zimri reigned seven days in Tirzah. Now the troops were encamped against Gibbethon, which belonged to the Philistines, and the troops who were encamped heard it said, 'Zimri has conspired, and he has killed the king.' Therefore all Israel made Omri, the commander of the army, king over Israel that day in the camp. So Omri went up from Gibbethon, and all Israel with him, and they besieged Tirzah. And when Zimri saw that the city was taken, he went into the citadel of the king's house and burned the king's house over him with fire and died." In 2 Samuel 17, we learn of yet another suicide, "Now it came to pass, after they had departed, that they came up out of the well and went and told King David, and said to David, 'Arise and cross over the water quickly. For thus has Ahithophel advised against you.' So David and all of the people who were with him arose and crossed over the Jordan. By morning light not one of them was left who had not gone over the Jordan. Now when Ahithophel saw this his advice was not followed, he saddled a donkey, and arose and went home to his house, to his city. Then put his household in order, and hanged himself, and died; and he was buried in his father' tomb" (21-23). Ahithophel had given treasonous information concerning David and his movements. When he was found out, he knew his fate and, as a result, he set his house in order and hanged himself.

There are only seven detailed accounts of suicide or possi-

THE CHRISTIAN AND GOOD MENTAL HEALTH

ble suicides in all of the Bible. We have noted each of these accounts. It is interesting that nowhere do we find a specific, direct condemnation of the act of suicide. I am certainly not promoting suicide or anyone ever taking their own life. Some say that suicide is self-murder, but this it not a correct definition of the word "murder." To murder is to take another's life, not one's own. Suicide is exclusively the taking of one's own life. Samson took his own life, yet is listed in the hall of the faithful (Hebrews 11:32). There are even situations where suicide may not be easily defined. Even today in our culture it may be difficult, a fine line between calling someone's death suicide or something else. There are Christians who were killed by ISIS because they refused to deny their faith in Jesus. They had the power over their own life. They could have denied Christ and saved their life. They chose to refuse to deny Jesus, though it meant instantaneous death, which says to me there are some things in this world worse than death. There are situations we are confronted with on occasion that are so spiritual in nature that when given the choice between instantly dying or denying the Lord, we would make the decision to die. It is true that we would not physically be taking our own life, but it is equally true that we have the power at that moment over our own life or death. We applaud people who are willing to die for their faith. We call them martyrs. Those Christians in the early days under Nero chose to go to the bear pits and the lion dens, to die rather than deny their faith in Jesus. What a powerful message that sends to the world. A martyr is a person who is willing to give their own life with full realization that their acknowledgement of faith will result in their death.

I personally believe there are things worse than death, and certainly the denial of God and our Lord is one of those things. Jesus, in John 10:17, 18, could have saved His own life. Jesus could have been spared the cross. It was within His own power to save His life. He had the power over His own life and death.

"For this reason the Father loves me, because I lay down my life that I may take it up again. No one takes it from me, but I lay it down of my own accord. I have authority to lay it down, and I have authority to take it up again. This charge I have received from my Father." Jesus could have caused ten thousand angels to sweep the whole howling mob into hell, but He didn't. He decided that there are things more valuable and more important than life. And so He chose to die. It could be said He came into the world for the specific, express purpose of dying, that it was His reason for living, dying for our sins.

Paul struggled with his own life and death issues on several occasions. There is little doubt in my mind that had a psychologist examined Paul he would have found him on occasion to be depressed. And why not, with all he had experienced? In Philippians 1:20, 21 Paul says, "...as it is my eager expectation and *hope* that I will not be at all ashamed, but that with full courage now as always Christ will be honored in my body, whether by life or by death. For to me to live is Christ, and to die is gain." Paul was saying that for him to continue to live was good for others, but he would rather go on and be at home with his Father. Verse 22: "If I am to live in the flesh, that means fruitful labor for me. Yet which I shall choose I cannot tell." Paul here is hovering between whether to go on to Heaven or to stay and be a blessing to others around him. He chose an unselfish route. The selfish way would have been to go ahead and be with the Father—to die. The unselfish choice was to continue to work, labor, and minister. Verse 23 says, " I am hard pressed between the two. My desire is to depart and be with Christ, for that is far better." Paul is saying that is the better thing for him. "But to remain in the flesh is more necessary on your account. Convinced of this, I know that I will remain and continue with you all, for your progress and joy in the faith" (Philippians 1:24, 25). That's what kept Paul alive and kept him going—to know that he was doing good for others. He would rather have died and gone to be with the Lord, but he stayed and helped others. "Hope is patience with the lamp lit" (Tertullian). "Hope lies in dreams, in imagination, and in the courage of those who dare to make dreams into reality" (Jonas Salk).

I have had many say that suicide is an unforgivable sin. I do not find that idea anywhere in the Scriptures. Some may begin the process of suicide and then wish they could reverse the process, but it is too late and they die. It is impossible for us to judge their eternal destiny, and I can find no Scripture directly stating that it is an unforgivable sin. If we are going to have to ask for specific forgiveness for every sin we may ever commit at the point of death, then there probably will be few people who are saved. All of us do things that we know are wrong, but maybe never get around to specifically asking for forgiveness for that sin. Is salvation like that? Is it up and down? I commit a sin, and I must specifically pray to God for forgiveness of that sin or I will be lost? I commit another sin and, unless I ask God specifically for the forgiveness of that sin and die, I will be lost. If it is up and down like that, I don't think there are many of us who have much hope of salvation. The Bible teaches us that the blood of Jesus Christ is continually cleansing us from all sins (1 John 1:7). That is very important. Salvation is not a yo-yo, and I suspect most people die having never specifically asked for forgiveness for a particular sin. I think it is a matter of the heart—our desire to do God's will always, but a realization that we often fall short. We ask God to forgive us always, and we are always sorry and repentant for what wrong we do.

What could we say about people who willingly give their lives for a cause, such as those who serve in the military or those who die for an affirmation of their faith? They choose to do it because they believe that some things are more important than life.

What about hospice? Hospice is a program that Donna (my

wife) and I have been involved with three times. Her father was diagnosed with advanced cancer. He had one radiation treatment and said, "I'll never take another." The doctor told him, "If you're willing to go through the chemo and radiation, we can almost guarantee you at least one more year of life. It could be as many as two or three." He said no, and hospice was called in. After a day or two, they gave him morphine, which caused him to become unconscious, and he died four days later. Was this suicide? He may have lived a little longer had he chosen the chemo and radiation route. His quality of life would have been poor, but there was the possibility he could have lived longer. He chose not to take advantage of what would have been a very painful and distasteful way of dying to him.

My mother, at 96, developed pneumonia. She had repeatedly said, "I'm ready to go," so my sisters and I had to make a difficult decision to grant her wishes. The doctor said she may live a short time longer, or she may die of the condition. But her choice, and it ended up being our choice, was hospice. She was administered morphine and soon lost consciousness. She passed away peacefully a few days later. Was this suicide? Should we have let nature take its course, even though it would have meant more pain and suffering for her with no assurance of longer life?

This brings us to another kind of what some call suicide, and that is older people who decide they want to die and simply quit eating. It might astound you how many make this decision to literally starve themselves to death. My wife's grandmother was a perfect example. She quit eating, and there was no way to force her to continue eating. The only option was a feeding tube. She maintained consciousness for a period of ten days, and then went into a coma. She was 97 years old, bedridden, in very bad health, and had made a conscious decision to take her own life through starvation. The death certificate gave the cause of death as "failure to thrive," but the failure to thrive was that she was ready to go. She had been asking to die. She told God she wanted to die. She said she was waiting only to die. She was ready to go, and so she in one sense took the situation into her own hands by refusing to eat. This phenomenon, when some people reach a certain stage in life and decide they just don't want to go on and quit eating, starving themselves to death, happens in all cultures throughout the world, and has been recorded throughout history. Is this suicide? Could it be defined as suicide? Even though it isn't an instantaneous act, it is an act that knowingly results in the death of the individual in a reasonably short time.

We need to be very careful in judging these decisions made by others. We cannot imagine the pain some people suffer continuously for months or even years—physical and emotional pain, from which there is little or no release. I am thankful that this decision is in God's hands as to the definition of suicide and the rightness or wrongness of it must be left to Him.

Early New Testament Christian disciples would greet each other with the word "Maranatha!" Maranatha means "Lord, come quickly. Lord, we hope You come today. Lord we hope we can go to be with You immediately." And just as we say, "Are you having a good day?" or "Have a good day," they would say "Maranatha! We hope today is the day the Lord comes." Possibly if our spirituality was what it should be, this would be our greeting as well.

Mary (names changed for confidentiality)

Mary would call Donna, my wife, every time there was a blood moon. If any one of you have ever seen a blood moon, you remember that it is spectacular and that there is a reference made to it in Revelation 6:12: "When he opened the sixth seal, I looked, and behold, there was a great earthquake, and the sun became black as sackcloth, the full moon became like blood." She would call and say, "Do you think the Lord might come today?" And she was excited about the possibility. "Do you think today might be the day? The moon is blood red!"

Mary had wanted to go to heaven for a long time. I would never judge any person who is experiencing pain of any kind—mental, physical, emotional. They are in God's hands, and that gives me comfort because I know God knows their heart and understands their motives. He understands all better than any of us ever will.

I hesitate to share this, but maybe I need to tell it as much as you may need to hear it. David, Mary's husband, called me a little over a week before her death. He said, "Mary isn't doing well at all. I think we need to talk immediately." That was on a Monday, and I set up a time to talk to them that day. When they arrived, and Mary walked in and sat down, I asked her only three questions and knew she had gone beyond where anyone needs to be in terms of their mental state and the value of their life. I turned to David and said, "We must put her in the hospital right now. We cannot wait." She was shaking her head no the whole time I was talking. I said, "David, I'm going to make arrangements to hospitalize her." So I called the local mental hospital and for the first time ever in maybe one hundred committals, I was able to get a bed on the first call. "Yes, there is a bed available. Make the referral and we'll expect her." At that point, we checked the insurance. Yes, insurance will pay for her stay, no problem. The whole time Mary was shaking her head no, and she had the most pained look on her face. So after all was ready and it was time to go, she said, "No, I'm not going. I have a doctor's appointment on Friday, and I want to go to that appointment." I said, "I don't want you to leave like this." She said again, "I'm not going to the hospital." So, reluctantly I made a safety plan with her. A safety plan is an agreement between a patient and a therapist, stating that the patient will not harm themselves. She agreed to the safety plan for one week. That is about as long ethically you can ask a person to agree to a safety plan.

I asked her to call me after her appointment on Friday. She

did, and told me that her doctor had given her medication. David and I tried to get her to come back to see me that day, but after her appointment with her primary care doctor she was content simply with a phone call. I recommended that she might want to go to Agape, a local mental health program, for counseling. I felt she might respond better to a female therapist rather than a male. An appointment was made at Agape, but when the time came for her to go, Mary refused. That was on the following Monday, one week after I initially met with her and tried to get her to go to the hospital. That was also the day that our safety plan ended. Two days later, on Wednesday night, I was teaching a class when the announcement came that she had taken her life. I don't think I have had anything affect me more powerfully that that event.

You may ask, "What would you have done differently?" I don't know, because if I had called an ambulance and the police and had her taken to the hospital by force, she would have told them, as she told me, "I don't have a specific plan to take my life." If you don't have a specific plan for suicide, it's difficult to be held against your will. Even if you are committed against your will, it is only for a period of 48-72 hours.

Mary was continually experiencing emotional pain, even from the first time that I counseled with her. I went back and thought through Mary's life. These are the words that came to me.

Mary was very caring and sensitive, very intuitive. She felt deeply, deeper than most. She experienced the world empathetically, where most of us see it sympathetically. She could actually put herself in the other person's place, feeling and literally empathizing with the feelings of the other person. She could feel their pain; she could know their discomfort and sorrow.

Mary saw beauty where few other people did. A rock was not just a rock to her. Wherever she went, when we were with her, she would collect rocks. On the Aegean Sea in Greece, she collected rocks from the shore. In each rock, she would see an individual beauty. She saw special beauty in lakes and mountains. She saw beauty in small trees and plants or small creatures. You and I would have possibly stepped on them. Mary, though, would pick small insects up, give them a kind of hug, and put them in a safe place.

Mary would internalize any criticism or negative comments she received. It made her sad and, in some ways, sick. She carried a heavy burden of other people's problems, difficulties, sicknesses, and sadnesses. She would put on a smile and would give you a big hug, but empathetically she was feeling very deeply for others. Inside she was sad, while outside she would be smiling. She would seldom disagree with people; she would seek to understand them. She would often say, "Why do they feel that way?" She would quietly try to understand their position, feeling others' guilt, others' pain, other's sorrows, others' sadness, even to the neglect of her own feelings and needs. She would take on the burdens of others.

Mary was a good soul, one of the better souls that I have ever known. She was in some ways a perfectionist living in a very imperfect world. The pain became so great and she started to starve herself. She had gone for ten days taking almost no nourishment at all, and that chemically affects the brain, causing the person not to think rationally. And then she chose to take her own life. I don't have all the answers, and your answers may be different than mine, but my belief, my conviction is that God understands such pain.

Questions

1. How many people in the United States attempt suicide each year?
2. How many people succeed in completing suicide each year?

3. What are six reasons given for suicide?

4. Discuss each of the biblical examples of suicide.

5. Are there things worse than death? What are some of them?

6. Do you believe that suicide is an unforgivable sin?

7. Could hospice be considered a form of consensual suicide?

8. Do you know someone who has completed suicide? What are your thoughts and feelings concerning their death?

CHAPTER 13

DEMONS AND EVIL SPIRITS —
NOT YOUR PROBLEM

Some may wonder why in a study of mental and emotional illness, we would have a chapter on demon possession and evil spirits. It is because I have found in over 30 years as a therapist there are Christians who feel, because of their guilt over a particular sin, that they may be demon-possessed or have an evil spirit, or have committed the unforgivable sin. People who are experiencing mental or emotional illness search for an explanation as to why it has happened to them. Just as many who are afflicted with diseases of one kind or another, or who have been involved in accidents which debilitate them, want to know why. Often we go to extremes in determining the reasons for the happenstances of life. Our reasons are often irrational.

No one today has the ability to diagnose evil spirits, or the ability to cast them out. Demon possession and evil spirits in the New Testament are not the same thing as mental or emotional illness today.

Having said that, there is a distinct difference between being demon-possessed and Satan-influenced. All of us are tempted and influenced by Satan. Demon possession involves a demon completely taking control of a person. Their thoughts and actions are all controlled by a demon. This is what happened in New Testament times. The Bible makes it clear that a person today cannot be demon possessed. We have free will. The plea of the gospel is "Whosoever will, let him take the water of life freely" (Revelation 22:17b, KJV). We can change our evil ways and be forgiven of our sins at any time in life.

Jesus Lives in Christians

A demon cannot live where Jesus lives. When one becomes a Christian, Jesus lives inside of him. The body becomes a temple of the Holy Spirit (1 Corinthians 3:16-17). The question is, "Do demons possess people today as they did in Jesus' day?" The gift of discerning the spirits and casting them out were a part of the signs, wonders, and miracles of Jesus, the apostles, and some early disciples. They were give to confirm the Word of God.

> ...how shall we escape if we neglect such a great salvation? It was declared at first by the Lord, and it was attested to us by those who heard, while God also bore witness by signs and wonders and various miracles and by gifts of the Holy Spirit distributed according to his will (Hebrews 2:3-4, ESV).

> And they went out and preached everywhere, while the Lord worked with them and confirmed the message by accompanying signs (Mark 16:20, ESV).

Authority to perform miracles was given by God through Jesus Christ, and it was given as He willed, to confirm His Son, the apostles and disciples of the first century, and to confirm the Word. Once the New Testament was completed, there was no longer a need for the miracles, signs, and wonders that were practiced in the first century. God inspired the writers so the Word is infallible, inerrant, and inspired. I have never known of anyone who has the authority or power to perform miracles and do the signs and wonders that Jesus, the apostles, or the early disciples did. There is no longer a need for these miracles, because we have an eyewitness account of what happened that has been inspired by God.

> ...just as those who from the beginning were eyewitnesses and ministers of the word have delivered them to us, it seemed good to me also, having followed all things closely for some time past, to write an orderly account for you, most excellent Theophilus, that you may have certainty concerning the things you have been taught (Luke 1:2-4, ESV).

God Will Take Care of His Children

There is no greater power in all of the world than the power of God as our protector. We may be Satan- and demon-oppressed, but not possessed. This condition is called temptation. We are all tempted in one way or another, at one time or another, to choose Satan's way over God's way. No one is beyond the power of Jesus to be forgiven of sins and be completely changed in their lives. The prodigal son is a perfect example of this. He went away, sunk as low as he could, hit rock bottom, and decided to return to the Father. A loving, patient, forgiving Father met him with open arms. So it is with each of us today. When we realize that what we have done is wrong, as children of God we repent, confess, and ask for forgiveness with the assurance that He will grant it.

Know Your Enemy

"...so that we would not be outwitted by Satan; for we are not ignorant of his designs" (2 Corinthians 2:11, ESV).

We must arm ourselves against Satan.

"Put on the whole armor of God, that you may be able to stand against the schemes of the devil" (Ephesians 6:11, ESV).

Satan can take on the appearance of an angel of light.

"And no wonder, for even Satan disguises himself as an angel of light" (2 Corinthians 11:14, ESV).

We must be careful not to ignore God's great truth and salvation.

"...how shall we escape if we neglect such a great salvation? It was declared at first by the Lord, and it was attested to us by those who heard, while God also bore witness by signs and wonders and various miracles and by gifts of the Holy Spirit distributed according to his will" (Hebrews 2:3, 4, ESV).

The devil always tries to hinder God's truth, and everything that is good and holy.

"The ones along the path are those who have heard; then the devil comes and takes away the word from their hearts, so that they may not believe and be saved" (Luke 8:12, ESV).

"And since they did not see fit to acknowledge God, God gave them up to a debased mind to do what ought not to be done. They were filled with all manner of unrighteousness, evil, covetousness, malice. They are full of envy, murder, strife, deceit, maliciousness. They are gossips, slanderers, haters of God, insolent, haughty, boastful, inventors of evil, disobedient to parents, foolish, faithless, heartless, ruthless. Though they know God's righteous decree that those who practice such things deserve to die, they not only do them but give approval to those who practice them" (Romans 1:28-32, ESV).

It is with our own free will, not by demon-possession, that we decide to serve either God or Satan. If we accept the grace of God, all can be forgiven. Temptation is not the same thing as demon-possession. The devil will lie to us and try to deceive us.

"You are of your father the devil, and your will is to do your father's desires. He was a murderer from the beginning, and does not stand in the *truth*, because there is no *truth* in him. When he lies, he speaks out of his own character, for he is a *liar* and the *father of lies*" (John 8:44, ESV).

We must always be on guard. We are all tempted and can be led astray.

"But each person is tempted when he is lured and enticed by his own desire" (James 1:14, ESV).

An Example

Two men are alcoholics. They both decide to quit drinking. One seeks the power of God, and then begins to do everything he can to eliminate the temptation from his life. He goes through the house and eliminates anything that would remind him of alcohol. He takes a different route home each day, choosing not to drive by the bars. He also chooses new friends, ones who do not abuse alcohol. He prays many times daily for strength and power to overcome his addiction, and he is able to remain faithful to his commitment.

The other man decides to quit on his own, but he continues with all of his old habits, making no effort to create new ones. He continues to go to the same places, with the same people, and expects different results. But it does not happen. Before long, this man is back drinking and his addiction is as powerful as ever.

The devil is called "the Tempter." He tempts us to do what is wrong, and what is not in our best interests, and sometimes to do what will eventually hurt us. He tempts us to do things that will harm us physically, mentally, and spiritually.

> "Watch and pray that you may not enter into temptation. The spirit indeed is willing, but the flesh is weak" (Matthew 26:41, ESV).

> "Be sober-minded; be watchful. Your adversary the devil prowls around like a roaring lion, seeking someone to devour. Resist him, firm in your faith, knowing that the same kinds of suffering are being experienced by your brotherhood throughout the world" (1 Peter 5:8, 9, ESV).

> "No temptation has overtaken you that is not common to man. God is faithful, and he will not let you be tempted beyond your ability, but with the temptation he will also provide the way of escape, that you may be able to endure it" (1 Corinthians 10:13, ESV).

God is faithful, and He will not let you be tempted beyond your ability to overcome. But with your temptation, He will provide an escape, so that you may be able to endure it. As children of God, we don't need a "no access" banner wrapped around us, or a sign that says "unfit for human habitation." We are children of God, of the King of kings and Lord of lords. We have been redeemed by the previous blood of Jesus; we have been bought with a price. Not with silver and gold, but with our own Savior's blood. Demons know and acknowledge that Jesus is the holy Son of God, and tremble (James 2:19). They know that they were defeated at the cross and at the resurrection. They know that one day they will be chained. No one is greater than God. He is our protector and Savior. Child of God, you cannot be demon possessed. You may have a mental or emotional problem, but it has nothing to do with demon possession as described in the early New Testament days. God loves you, and He will give you the grace to bear whatever burden you have.

Demons and Evil Spirits

> And they went into Capernaum, and immediately on the Sabbath he entered the synagogue and was teaching. And they were astonished at his teaching, for he taught them as one who had authority, and not as the scribes. And immediately there was in their synagogue a man with an unclean spirit. And he cried out, "What have you to do with us, Jesus of Nazareth? Have you come to destroy us? I know who you are—the Holy One of God." But Jesus rebuked him, saying, "Be silent, and come out of him!" And the unclean spirit, convulsing him and crying out with a loud voice, came out of him. And they were all amazed, so that they questioned among themselves, saying, "What is this? A new teaching with authority! He commands even the unclean spirits, and they obey him." And at once his fame spread everywhere throughout all the surrounding region of Galilee (Mark 1:21-28, ESV).

In the later verses, it says Jesus went into the synagogue and healed many who were physically ill and possessed with demons and spirits. Let's trace for a few moments the beginning of the ministry of Jesus. We follow His life from His baptism, to His temptation, to the beginning of His ministry in Judea, His ministry in Samaria, until He finally arrives in Galilee. There He goes to His hometown of Nazareth. He was not born there, but He did spend most of His youth in Nazareth. As Jesus visited there, people would say, "That's just Jesus. We've known Him since He was a child." And they did not and would not accept Him as being who He really was: the Son of God. As a result, Jesus went to Capernaum. One of the great privileges of Donna's and my life was being able to visit these places. We spent several days in Nazareth and then visited Capernaum. Capernaum was the home of Peter, Andrew, James, and John. Capernaum came as close to the earthly home of Jesus as He ever had. He went to the shore of the Sea of Galilee saying, "Follow me, and I will make you become fishers of men" (Mark 1:17, ESV). That began the ministry of Jesus.

> Now when the sun was setting, all those who had any who were sick with various diseases brought them to him, and he laid his hands on every one of them and healed them. And demons also came out of many, crying, "You are the Son of God!" But he rebuked them and would not allow them to speak, because they knew that he was the Christ (Luke 4:40, 41, ESV).

Understanding Life and Death

I have spoken and written many times about death, but there was something surreal as I sat next to my mother's bed, knowing she was dying. I watched her chest as it went up and down. Then, it stopped. There was no more breathing. I turned to Donna and said, "She's gone." The Spirit had left the body. The body that was there before me was no longer *the person who had inhabited it*. There lived in that body a spirit. In fact, that body just housed the most important part of my mother, her spirit.

We all have a spirit. The spirit, as it leaves the body, lives eternally. The spirit is much more valuable than the body. Yet we spend most of our time preoccupied with the physical body, and we often neglect the unseen eternal soul. That's where we should be placing most of our effort and attention, but like so many, the tangible becomes what is most important to us. I cannot see your soul. I can, however, see the fruit of your spirit. I can see how you behave and live, and know what is in control of your life and what spirit lives in you—whether the spirit of God or the spirit of Satan.

We have very broad principles to guide and lead us through this maze we call life, with all of its difficulties, pits, and traps. When we are baptized we are told that we receive the Holy Spirit as a gift (Acts 2:38). That means Christians have something that non-Christians do not have. We have an advantage. We have God's Spirit as a helper to remain faithful.

Jewish Tradition About Evil Spirits

Jewish people use the Talmud, which is a collection of oral traditions. There are two accounts—the Jerusalem Talmud and the Babylonian Talmud. In these two books, we find many demonic superstitions, ranging from black cats to walking under a ladder. This was a part of the interpretations of the Scriptures and oral traditions during and after the time of Jesus. They are all superstition. The Talmud is not inspired. The Apocrypha books, such as the Wisdom of Solomon, are not inspired. In the Wisdom of Solomon much is said about demon possession and exorcism.

It is amazing how many people believe these ideas. According to the Talmud, the way that evil spirits came about was that Eve cohabited with another spirit male, and Adam cohabited with another spirit female. As a result, all evil spirits came into the world. These evil spirits began to multiply and take over people's lives. The supposed goddess of the evil spirits was named Lilith. The god of the evil spirits was called Amagosh. Many early Jews believed this is where evil spirits originated.

> Then some of the itinerant Jewish exorcists undertook to invoke the name of the Lord Jesus over those who had evil spirits, saying, "I adjure you by the Jesus whom Paul proclaims." Seven sons of a Jewish high priest named Sceva were doing this. But the evil spirit answered them, "Jesus I know, and Paul I recognize, but who are you?" And the man in whom was the evil spirit leaped on them, mastered all of them and overpowered them,

so that they fled out of that house naked and wounded. And this became known to all the residents of Ephesus, both Jews and Greeks. And fear fell upon them all, and the name of the Lord Jesus was extolled. Also many of those who were now believers came, confessing and divulging their practices. And a number of those who had practiced magic arts brought their books together and burned them in the sight of all. And they counted the value of them and found it came to fifty thousand pieces of silver. So the word of the Lord continued to increase and prevail mightily (Acts 19:13-20, ESV).

Magicians were doing this according to Jewish trickery. They had been casting out in the name of demons. They would say, "I adjure you in the name of Bentit, Bentima, Carezma, Marigog, and Estagog. Come out, evil spirits!" So these Jews who were making a living by supposedly casting out evil spirits with these incantations decided that Paul and Jesus were having far greater success than they were. They substituted demon names with the names of Jesus and Paul. What happened? The spirits beat them.

When Jesus was tempted by Satan all His responses began with, "It is written." The problem today is that we don't know the Word well enough to deflect these attempts by Satan, so we often believe the lies. The Bible says that Satan is the father of lies. All he has to do is change one or two words or say, "That's not wrong, and if you do it, you'll become as wise as God." What can we do to arm ourselves against the devil and his lies? We must know God's Word. Put on God's armor and fight daily. Only then will we be protected.

But I say, walk by the Spirit, and you will not gratify the desires of the flesh. For the desires of the flesh are against the Spirit, and the desires of the Spirit are against the flesh, for these are opposed to each other, to keep you from doing the things you want to do. But if you are led by the Spirit, you are not under the law. Now the works of the flesh are evident: sexual immorality, impurity, sensuality, idolatry, sorcery, enmity, strife, jealousy, fits of anger, rivalries, dissensions, divisions, envy, drunkenness, orgies, and things like these. I warn you, as I warned you before, that those who do such things will not inherit the kingdom of God. But the fruit of the Spirit is love, joy, peace, patience, kindness, goodness, faithfulness, gentleness, self-control; against such things there is no law. And those who belong to Christ Jesus have crucified the flesh with its passions and desires.

If we live by the Spirit, let us also keep in step with the Spirit. Let us not become conceited, provoking one another, envying one another. (Galatians 5:16-26, ESV)

If God's Spirit is in you, you are protected and encapsulated by the mercy and grace of Almighty God. That's a most comforting thought.

Questions

1. Do people today have the ability to diagnose evil spirits or the ability to cast them out if they exist?

2. Discuss the difference between being demon possessed and Satan influenced.

3. Why was the ability to perform miracles part of the early New Testament history? Why were the apostles and certain disciples given the ability to heal?

4. Does being a Christian automatically prohibit us from becoming mentally ill or from having physical illnesses and difficulties?

5. According to the Talmud, how did evil spirits come into the world?

6. Discuss the mystery of our spirit or soul. Which is more important—our soul, or our body? Why?

7. What do we spend most of our time and effort pleasing, the body or the soul?

8. What are some advantages that Christians have that non-Christians to not in overcoming the problems, difficulties, and temptations of this life?

9. When Jesus was tempted, what was His first response to Satan with each temptation?

10. Discuss Galatians 5:16-26 and how it relates to us living in the Spirit and overcoming temptation.

POSTSCRIPT

We live in an ever-changing world, but nothing is changing any more quickly than our moral and ethical values. These changes are filtering into the areas of mental and emotional health. An example can be seen in the changes in the diagnosis of gays and lesbians, or homosexuals. Prior to 1973, homosexuality was considered to be abnormal behavior under Section 302 of the DSM II. This section was labeled "Sexual Deviation." In 1973, after much political pressure as well as pressure from within, the American Psychiatric Association decided to remove homosexuality from the DSM and say that it does not need any treatment and is to be considered as a normal lifestyle.

This change shows us how diagnostic mental and emotional health issues have changed. Even in our current culture we find another area of significant change. For many years, delusional behavior was diagnosed and treated as a mental and emotional disorder. However, in recent times delusion seems to be more and more accepted. Recent examples: a lady who is white and has been determined to be white from biologic tests, says she is black. She identifies completely with the black culture, though her parents both say she is white and that there is no indication of her being black. She has adopted black styles and dialect, and in every way considers herself black. Does the fact that she identifies herself as black mean that she is and should be accepted as black? Or should this be considered delusional thinking?

Another example: a man believes that he was born with two arms, but should have been born with only one. Therefore he has one arm amputated, for no other reason than he believes that he was meant to live with one arm in this life. Should that behavior and thinking be condoned, or should it be defined as delusional?

Another example: a 12-year-old female presents herself to the therapist and states that she is male. She believes she is male, she dresses and acts as a male, and when she is old enough she intends to have surgery and hormones which will allow her to appear more male. Should this thinking and behavior be accepted, or should therapists try to reason with her that she was born female in every biological way and that this is her destiny? Is her thinking delusional, or should it be considered rational?

Another example: a person who is black perceives themselves to be white, and believes they are white, even going to the extent of bleaching their skin and having multiple facial surgeries to appear more Caucasian. Does this belief or affirmation on their part make them white, or is it simply delusional?

When I was doing an internship, we regularly visited mental hospitals. There were many people in those hospitals who believed that they were Napoleon or George Washington or Elvis. They held this belief firmly, and adjusted their lifestyle to this identity belief, even going so far as to dress and speak as these historical figures did. We classify that person as being delusional, because we realize they are not Napoleon, or George Washington, or Elvis. And yet today, in modern mental and emotional health areas, many therapists are simply telling delusional patients, "Embrace your delusions. Live your delusions. Accept your delusions." Is this reasonable therapy for delusional people? Or should these people be diagnosed as being delusional and treated for their delusions?

Our world is changing rapidly and we have to be very aware of the direction that we are going and the consequences of that direction. In my experience, those who tried to change their identity, sometimes going to extraordinary lengths such as surgery, had not found the peace that they had hoped for, despite their best efforts to become who they thought they were.

Perception may be reality in the mind of certain individuals, but false perception is not reality. When we accept and encourage delusion as being a reasonable mental condition, then we may find this acceptance is worse than the delusional disorder and creates more problems than it solves. I encourage everyone to carefully analyze the changing conditions of our modern culture and society, apply common sense and reasoning to the many changes that are taking place in every area, including mental and emotional health, and understand that perception is not always reality.

HOTLINE AND INFORMATION PHONE NUMBERS

▶ **National Suicide Prevention Hotline**
1-800-273-8255

▶ **Samaritan's Helpline**
212-673-3000

▶ **Addiction Treatment Resource and Helpline**
877-999-6466 (information line)
844-278-9300 (helpline)

For immediate help in a mental health crisis, call 911 or go to your nearest emergency room. Most local counties have mental health crisis response teams which can be accessed through your local emergency room or 911 service.

BIBLIOGRAPHY

Anderson, Scott. "The Urge to End It All." *www.nytimes.com*. accessed June 30, 2015. http://www.nytimes.com/2008/07/06/magazine/06suicide-t.html?pagewanted=all&_r=0

Ashmore, Margaret. *Depression: The Sun Always Rises*. Phillipsburg, NJ: P & R Publishing, 2013.

Axelrod, Julie. "The 5 Stages of Loss and Grief." *www.psychcentral.com*. accessed July 27, 2015. http://psychcentral.com/lib/the-5-stages-of-loss-and-grief/.

Bryan, Alan M. *Climb Happiness Hill*. Lubbock, TX: Sunset Institute Press, 2012.

Criswell, W.A. "Grief At the Death of Family/Friends." *www.wacriswell.com*. accessed June 20, 2015. www.wacriswell.com/sermons/1958/grief-at-the-death-of-family-friends/.

Czikszentmihlyi, Mihaly. *Flow: The Psychology of Optimal Experience*. New York: Harper Perennial Modern Classics, 2008.

Deschene, Lori. "Dealing With Regret: 8 Ways to Benefit and Move Forward." *www.tinybuddha.com*. accessed October 29, 2015. http://tinybuddha.com/blog/dealing-with-regret-8-ways-to-benefit-and-move-forward/.

Grant, Dave. *The Ultimate Power*. Old Tappan, NJ: Fleming H. Revell, 1983.

Hay, Louise, and David Kessler. *You Can Heal Your Heart*. Carlsbad, CA: Hay House Inc., 2014.

Holtrop, Cindy. "Psalm 88." (sermon at Calvin CRC, Grand Rapids MI. April 25, 2010)

Hopler, Whitney. "Avoid the Dumb Mistakes Christians Make." *www.crosswalk.com*. accessed October 29, 2015. http://www.crosswalk.com/faith/spiritual-life/avoid-the-dumb-mistakes-christians-make-1407861.html.

_____. "Avoid the Top Ten Mistakes College Students Make." *www.crosswalk.com*. accessed October 29, 2015. http://www.crosswalk.com/family/career/avoid-the-top-ten-mistakes-college-students-make.html.

Hunt, June. *Depression: Walking From Darkness Into the Dawn.* Torrance, CA: Aspire Press, 2013.

_____. *Fear: No Longer Afraid.* Torrance, CA: Aspire Press, 2013.

_____. *Suicide Prevention.* Torrance, CA: Aspire Press, 2013.

Insel, Thomas R., Pamela Y. Collins, and Steven E. Hyman. "Darkness Invisible: The Hidden Global Costs of Mental Illness." *Foreign Affairs,* January/February 2015, 127.

Jackson, Wayne. *The Bible and Mental Health.* Courier Publications, 1998.

Kubler-Ross, Elisabeth, and David Kessler. *On Grief and Grieving.* New York: Scribner, 2005.

Lewis, C.S. *Mere Christianity.* London: Macmillan, 1978.

Lickerman, Alex. "The Six Reasons People Attempt Suicide." *www.psychologytoday.com.* accessed June 30, 2015. https://www.psychologytoday.com/blog/happiness-in-world/201004/the-six-reasons-people-attempt-suicide.

Lyubomirsky, Sonja. *The How of Happiness: A New Approach to Getting the Life You Want.* New York: Penguin Press, 2008.

Meyer, Tony. "Light For a Dark Path." *www.thebanner.org.* accessed March 17, 2016. http://www.thebanner.org/features/2011/01/light-for-a-dark-path.

Minirth, Frank B., and Paul D. Meier. *Happiness Is a Choice.* Grand Rapids, MI: Baker Book House, 1978.

Paquette, Jonah. *Real Happiness.* Eau Claire, WI: PESI Publishing, 2015.

"Practical Ways to Approach Your Grief." *www.hynesmemorial.org.* accessed October 29, 2015. http://www.hynesmemorial.org/grief-support/practical-ways-approach-your-grief.

Provance, Jake, and Keith Provance. *Keep Calm and Trust God.* Tulsa, OK: Word and Spirit Publishing, 2014.

Seligman, Martin. *Authentic Happiness: Using the New Positive Psychology to Realize Your Potential for Lasting Fulfillment.* New York: Atria Books, 2004.

_____. Learned Optimism: *How to Change Your Mind and Your Life.* New York: Vintage Books, 2006.

Smedes, Lewis B. "Is Suicide Unforgivable?" www.christianitytoday.com. accessed June 20, 2015. http://www.christianitytoday.com/ct/2000/july10/30.61.html.

Smith, Laura L., and Charles H. Elliott. *Anxiety & Depression for Dummies*. Hoboken, NJ: Wiley Publishing, 2006.

Sternberg, Barbara. "Understanding Anxiety." *Institute For Natural Resources Health Update*. September 2010.

"Strong Emotions." Alive Hospice Grief Support.

"Suicide." *www.wikipedia.org*. accessed July 27, 2015. https://en.wikipedia.org/wiki/Suicide.

"Suicide Warning Signs." *www.afsp.org*. accessed July 27, 2015. https://www.afsp.org/preventing-suicide/suicide-warning-signs.

Swaim, Larry. "The Error Chain." (sermon, July 2015, derived from idea by Tommy Colyar)

Walmsley, Lesley, comp. *C.S. Lewis on Grief*. Nashville, TN: Thomas Nelson Publishers, 1998.

Walton, Charlie. *Twelve Faces of Grief*. St. Meinrad, IN: One Caring Place/Abbey Press, 1998.

_____. *When There Are No Words*. Ventura, CA: Pathfinder Publishing of California, 1996.